ROUTLEDGE LIBRARY EDITIONS:
RESPONDING TO FASCISM

THE SPANISH TRAGEDY

THE SPANISH TRAGEDY

JEF LAST

Translated from the Dutch by
DAVID HALLETT

Volume 7

LONDON AND NEW YORK

First published in English 1939

This edition first published in 2010
by Routledge
2 Park Square, Milton Park, Abingdon, Oxon, OX14 4RN

Simultaneously published in the USA and Canada
by Routledge
52 Vanderbilt Avenue, New York, NY 10017

Routledge is an imprint of the Taylor & Francis Group, an informa business

First issued in paperback 2013

British Library Cataloguing in Publication Data
A catalogue record for this book is available from the British Library

ISBN 13: 978-0-415-57699-4 (Set)
eISBN 13: 978-0-203-85012-1 (Set)

ISBN 13: 978-0-415-85306-4 (pbk) (Volume 7)
ISBN 13: 978-0-415-58012-0 (hbk) (Volume 7)
ISBN 13: 978-0-203-85018-3 (ebk) (Volume 7)

Jef Last

THE SPANISH TRAGEDY

Translated from the Dutch by
DAVID HALLETT

LONDON
GEORGE ROUTLEDGE & SONS, LTD.
BROADWAY HOUSE: 68–74 CARTER LANE, E.C.

De Spaansche Tragedie first published in Holland 1938
The Spanish Tragedy first published, 1939

Printed in Great Britain by Butler & Tanner Ltd., Frome and London

CONTENTS

INTRODUCTION

I HAVE SET MYSELF A DIFFICULT TASK. NOW THAT events in Spain have taken a tragic turn, I feel the need to record my own general view of the course of these events, by way of conclusion to the happenings and experiences that were my portion in the struggle.

Where it is a question of discussing the arming and remodelling of the army, the courage of the comrades in the trenches, the sufferings of the civilian population, the magnificent cultural achievements of the Government, or the miracle of the latent forces which have now grown active in the Spanish people, I feel I can speak with expert knowledge, because I experienced and lived through it all.

But to discuss the political situation is a different matter. I fear that you can barely realize the isolation of an officer's existence at the front, how little he knows of the general military operations even a few kilometres away. News of the outer world filters through to him in censored newspapers, which he can only come by at irregular intervals ; his judgment is inevitably influenced by the political composition of the unit in which he has to live. He obtains his view of the world from what he has more or less accidentally heard or read ; he lacks the time for systematic investigation and for properly checking the various rumours that reach him. Conscious of these limitations, I have until now confined myself in all I have said and written to recording exclusively what I saw with my own eyes.

If, nevertheless, I have now been able to form a general picture of the course of events, I am aware that this picture should not be considered a final appraisement, since it is necessary still to check it in all its details. I was not placed like so many journalists in the very centre of events. While they could actually see the threads being woven, my view was that of the man in the street, my eyes those of a soldier in the trenches. I had, however, a few advantages which all did not possess. I could read and understand Castilian very well, and at a later stage was able also to read the Catalan press. I lived among working-class families of all political opinions and at the Alianza met Spanish artists and intellectuals of every school. In the Gran Via I came upon foreign journalists. Repeatedly I was the guest of the Russian delegation in Gailord, and during the writers' congress in Madrid I had many conversations with the leading literary figures from South America and Europe.

It is not, however, as an intellectual but as a front-line soldier that I wish to approach the Spanish problem, and in this connection the first point I should like to stress is the great contrast existing between the spirit at the front and the spirit behind the lines. Among the men in the trenches considerable indignation is aroused by the political game that goes on behind the front. Rightly or wrongly the soldiers at the front have the impression that all who were truly sincere in their convictions enlisted in the very first days of the war, and that political conflicts behind the front are fanned and kept in being by the politicians, who see in the continuation of these conflicts a *raison d'être* for their own existence and the chance of not being sent to the front themselves. Communal life in the trenches tends to blur and eliminate all original political divergences ; only the will to victory endures and the general attitude of the front-line soldiers can be summarized in the words of Durutti : "We are prepared if necessary to lose everything except the war."

In many cases the men in the trenches, that is to say the common people, the ordinary workers, peasants, and lower middle class of Spain belong to this or that party ; but this is not to say that they know or understand the party programme. Looking beyond the slogans which they have adopted and made their own, it will be seen that in their hearts they have no economic or political system but exclusively a number of reasonable wishes common to all mankind.

These wishes, however, are much less determined by direct economic interests than is generally assumed. The worker whose only ambition it would be to live like a petit bourgeois would not hold out for months on end in the lousy depths of a trench. The peasant who was only thinking of obtaining a better existence for himself would not be prepared of his own volition to risk his skin every day of his life. Whoever attempts to capture the youth of a country by speculating exclusively upon its desires, its pleasures, and its diversions, is playing a losing game, for it is only by courage and by sacrifice, by discarding its own interests, that youth can prove its worth to itself and to the outside world. The hatred of " rational pacifism " evinced by young men is to be explained by the fact that these pacifists are speculating upon their fears and cowardice. Similarly a boy who is worth his salt kicks against the pricks when his father endeavours to demonstrate on rational grounds that it will be more to his advantage to enter a grocer's business than for him to take up an artistic profession in which hunger may be his only reward.

The proletariat are the youth of mankind: they have yet to prove their worth to themselves and their fellow men. This is precisely what differentiates the Stakhanov worker, exalted into a socialist hero, from the true, unknown socialist heroes in prison and concentration camps, on the barricades and in the trenches : the behaviour of the latter is irrational to this extent, that their deeds do not bring personal advantage or preferred treatment, but the very opposite.

Undoubtedly the Spanish worker was confident that after victory his family would endure less hunger and be better housed than in the old days, that his children would have the prospect of a better future ; but his hatred of the landlord living in a palace surrounded by the hovels of the poor does not, as the bourgeoisie imagines, spring from the wish that he himself should also live in such a palace—you should have heard the remarks of my peasant boys when I took them round the palace of the Alianza ! It is much more a moral hatred originating in an outraged sense of justice that refuses to tolerate such a distinction on grounds of human dignity. If my peasants from Jaen shot down their master, it was not because he exploited them, but because he "just damn well wouldn't ever speak to them personally," but insisted upon replying to them only through his secretary.

Behind all the political camouflage, what these people really want is simply more love, more liberty, more justice, more culture, and a little less hunger.

It seems to me that, buried deep beneath social and political theories, the actual wishes of the masses are of a fairly moderate nature, and could be satisfied within the limits of a democratic republic, in which the forces of production and the resources of the soil were developed along modern lines. The practice of a democracy enjoying political freedom, labour protection, and a level of existence such as one meets with in Norway, for instance, would undoubtedly seem paradise on earth to the overwhelming majority of soldiers who are now manning the trenches in Spain.

One morning in November 1936, while we were stationed in the half-destroyed suburb of Carabanchel, I arrived at the house occupied by our captain Pepe. A framed print, purporting to represent the Republic, was still hanging over the front door : a comely Spanish maiden flanked by a lion and a tricolour. To my astonishment the national emblem had been entirely riddled with bullets, although at that angle they could not have come from the enemy.

In my amazement I asked Captain Pepe, who was twenty-one and a Communist, for an explanation. With a smile he pointed to his revolver: "I had to try the new thing out."—"But, Pepe, have you gone quite mad? Fancy shooting at the Republic!"

"Come, come," said Pepe, "*esta vieja puta*—that old whore—is nothing but the Bourgeois Republic!"

Now my point in relating this incident is that such an attitude on the part of a Communist or an officer of the Republic is quite unthinkable to-day, after eighteen months of civil war. The Communists themselves have been responsible for introducing everywhere the flag parade with the salute to the tricolour; at their meetings their commissars only speak of the defence of the Republic and never at any time of the social revolution. What is more, among the men themselves this new terminology has also found general acceptance.

There was a time when the Communist slogan "We want a *parliamentary*, democratic republic of a new type," met with great opposition, especially among the youth associations. As everywhere else, parliamentarism derived its main support from the middle class of the Left; it had been fundamentally compromised in the eyes of the youth of the country, whose only experience of it had been accompanied by unemployment and misery. The latter's wishes were all for a more thorough-going democracy and were expressed in such slogans as " Self-government by the effective organized units," " Syndicalist Federalism," " Government by Councils," or " Dictatorship of the Proletariat." It is a fact that in the army, at any rate, such slogans have almost ceased to be heard even in private conversation, and that even the qualification " of a new type," attached to the conception of a democratic republic, is now usually dropped. A cursory glance at the country's recent history will go some way to explain this fairly drastic change in the feelings of the masses.

When in 1931 the King fled the country, the situation that ensued bore not the least resemblance to a socialist revolution. What occurred was merely the collapse of a feudal régime which had gone entirely bankrupt and had foundered on the shoals of its own rottenness. Bolstered up by the Church, Feudalism had maintained itself longer in Spain than anywhere else in Europe. It had been successful in acting as a complete brake to progress ; neither industry nor agriculture was able to develop. The country's mineral resources had fallen into foreign hands, and it was no accident that an autonomous movement grew stronger every day among the middle classes in Catalonia and the Basque country, the two economically most developed portions of the country. At long last the Spanish middle class wished to assume its place in the sun. However, as was also the case with Russia during the world war, evolution had already reached the stage when the middle class was able to achieve its object only with the assistance of the revolutionary proletariat. No wonder that, like Goethe's magician, it soon grew afraid of the forces it had unleashed, and that in the process the bourgeois "fathers of the republic," Zamora, Dr. Marañan, and even Colonel Franco fell back one by one into the bosom of reaction. It should be noted, besides, that the broad masses of the Spanish people were culturally backward, and that a typically Spanish romantic anarchism had grown up on this soil. While anarchism in Catalonia had its philosophy, its organizations, its newspapers, and very able leaders, it must be conceded that a considerable proportion of the peasants wore their anarchism with a difference. In the main it was a blend of hatred of the oppressors, feelings of revenge, and dreams of a millennium. During the first years of the Republic this anarchism unwittingly played into the hands of reaction by its assumption of an ultra-Left attitude. By not taking part in the elections, and by refusing on principle all share in the Government, it was instrumental in bringing the reactionary Leroux Government into power, and, by its indifference to the Catalan revolt, it assumed another grave responsibility. Consequently, Marxist groups, though originally very weak, were gradually able, especially in Madrid, to assume the leadership of the proletariat, particularly when, by responding to what was felt by the masses to be a necessity, they proclaimed the united front. Broadened out into a popular front these tactics provided the basis of the electoral victory of 1936 and the constitution of the Azaña Government.

From the very beginning this weak and faltering and purely bourgeois Government was not popular with the masses. As was also the case in France, the Left parties within the Popular Front were the prisoners of the Right wing. It was found impossible to carry out thorough-going reforms within the frame-work of the bourgeois republic.

The Government was accepted and supported as the only possible concentration for defence against the rising tide of Fascism, but the positive results achieved were thought to be anything but satisfactory.

When the explosion occurred—which Azaña by his moderation had made every effort to prevent—and the generals broke their oath to the constitution, the weakness of the Government was suddenly revealed in all its nakedness. To maintain its authority it had neither a police force nor an army at its disposal. Then it was that the hastily armed working-class, without officers, without plans, without artillery, destroyed the Fascists in the principal towns of the country, and, proceeding with all speed to the mountains, held up the approach of the oncoming Fascist hordes. It was no wonder that in those days the people considered themselves entitled to make demands that far outran the moderate plans of the original Government. At that time it looked as if Spain stood on the threshold of a revolutionary development, and as if the war could be conducted as a revolutionary war. It was then a fairly common view that a new and attractive type of labour movement was about to arise from the fusion of an individualistic and anarchistic sense of freedom with Communist discipline, on the various fronts and in the factory committees themselves. And, indeed, at political gatherings such as were then usual, even in the army, it did seem as if a healthy fusion of the various groups would in practice be evolved.

These expectations were not fulfilled. Although negotiations for a united front took place between Durutti and Rosenberg, the Communists, as was always the case, had in mind only a united front in which they themselves were the officers and the others provided the soldiers. While not wishing to apportion the blame for what ensued, it must be placed on record that the tragedy of Germany was here repeated. Just as in that country Social Democrats and Communists were unable to come together, here too it was found impossible to constitute a united front between the two really big groups into which the proletariat of Spain were divided. This tragic fact has lengthened the struggle in Spain for at least a year, has cost hundreds of thousands of human lives, and finally brought the Fascists into Catalonia. At the same time it must be conceded that it was very difficult to find the basis for a really genuine united front.

The existing contrasts can best be shown by letting the leaders of the two extreme groups speak for themselves.

In December 1936 the Central Committee of the P.O.U.M. published the following proclamation, quoted in Trond Hegna's *Spanias Frihetskamp*, pp. 98–9: "A democratic parliament is an institution that accords with the period before July 19th. Neither by its composition nor by its nature can it fulfil the revolutionary demands of the present. The new society cannot be created by any parliament, but only by a constituent assembly, on the basis of a Spain liberated from landowners and capitalists. This constituent assembly cannot be elected by universal suffrage, which is a relic of bourgeois democracy; the delegates must be representatives of factory, worshop, and peasant committees, supplemented by representatives from the fronts. This assembly must take the initiative in transforming the country along socialist lines and be led by a government of workers and peasants representing the broad masses of the people who are struggling against Fascism and who are not spilling their blood for a democratic republic, but for a society that has been liberated from capitalist exploitation."

On the other hand, in January 1937 Juan Comorera, on behalf of the central committee of the P.S.U.C. (the United Social Democratic Party of Catalonia), spoke as follows : " The United Socialist Party of Catalonia is struggling for a democratic and parliamentary republic. The bourgeoisie of the whole world has ceased to have confidence in parliamentary institutions and a systematic campaign to discredit them has already begun. There are workers who have come under the influence of this campaign to discredit parliament. It goes without saying that our democratic and parliamentary republic will assume a different character from that which obtained when it still bore the traditional seal of privileged great landowners and big financiers. In our democratic and parliamentary republic, the labouring masses of the people will have the effective right to dispose of the country's destiny. There will be no room here for an outlawed Fascism whose material foundations we shall have destroyed.

"Spain is an economically undeveloped country, and subject to a considerable extent to the world market. The industries of Catalonia are very greatly dependent upon imports. Catalonia has practically no raw materials, and even its coal must be imported from England. In these circumstances peaceful co-operation with those countries in the world which are on a friendly footing with Spain is an absolutely vital necessity. The P.S.U.C. does not repudiate its socialist objectives, but it is conscious of its heavy responsibility towards the whole nation in making sure of victory in this war. And if we are to win this war we must guard against provoking the enmity of the democratic States when we already have to deal with Fascist intervention. The territorial, international, and political situation of Spain is entirely different from that of Russia during the great revolution, and a policy which takes no account of geographical and international factors must of necessity lead to defeat."

New and attractive forms of self-government had already arisen among the working-class in Catalonia ; how excellently they functioned within their scope—how much better than the old State apparatus with its spies, saboteurs, and bureaucrats—can be read in Jean Richard Bloch's *Espagne, Espagne !*

Indeed, a way seemed to be opened that might have led to the gradual dissolution of the State. I myself was never in Catalonia, but, particularly since I left Spain, conversations with many comrades who fought there, and books such as Bertram D. Wolfe's extremely instructive *Civil War in Spain* have convinced me that the activities of the Anarchists, which in the Communist press of Madrid were perpetually represented to us in a comical light, were actually among the most interesting and notable creations of the entire civil war. At the same time it is a fact that there was no common ground between the P.O.U.M. and the Anarchists upon which to base a line of action. While the P.O.U.M. wanted councils, the C.N.T. wanted trade union committees and a trade union government. These trade union committees usually meant in practice that groups of workers received preferred treatment at the expense of the public. Against the P.O.U.M., whose leaders Maurin and Nin were being vilified and attacked in all manner of ways by Trotsky, were also ranged the Trotskyites with their paper *La Voz Leninista*.

But even more important than the theoretical views are the practical objections raised by Camorera.

Even during the most favourable period of the struggle, there was one unalterable geographical factor : only one hundred and fifty kilometres separated Teruel from the coast. On the Madrid front a break-through of fifteen kilometres might have been decisive. Every hold-up in industry, transport, or food supply might be fatal. Furthermore, the peasants themselves were anything but keen upon those experiments which had been tried here and there ; there was a lack of intellectuals ; there was no point in offending the lower middle classes, which in Spain were in any case revolutionary by tradition ; finally, active intervention on England's part against a Soviet Spain would have spelt the end.

If one wished to dabble in historical hypotheses, it might be possible to maintain that a revolutionary course of events would have been feasible in Spain, if Fascism had been definitely overthrown during the first weeks. It may be that the great Powers, confronted by a *fait accompli*, would no more have ventured to intervene than when confronted by the *faits accomplis* of the Fascist revolutions. But such a victory over an organized army would only have been possible, if, over and above revolutionary enthusiasm, we had also had at our disposal other weapons than those with which we were supplied by Mexico during those first months. In other words, it would only have been possible if the Soviet Union had come to the aid of the Republic with the same temerity and insolence which were evinced from the very first moment by the Fascists in coming to the rescue of their kindred brethren. The Soviet Union, however, had no thought of pursuing such a policy. In the first place it was not interested in a revolutionary course of events which was diametrically opposed to the reactionary tendencies which were now gaining the upper hand in Russia itself. In the second place, such a policy would have disrupted the alliance with France. And, thirdly, it might have drawn the Soviet Union into a new world war, in which the most unfavourable combination of world powers would have been ranged against Moscow. Besides, the geographical connection between the Soviet Union and Spain was dominated by Italy and an increasingly lukewarm Turkey.

When we visited the Soviet Union in July 1936 we noted with much indignation a complete lack of interest in the events of Spain. They were not discussed at any gathering, and when the subject was broached in any private conversation, an expression of personal opinions seemed to be anxiously avoided. But it is also true that when towards the end of August the word finally went round in the press to support Spain, incredible enthusiasm was evinced by the Russian people. For a long time, however, the assistance afforded remained as purely philanthropical as that of the Second International. The *Komsomol*, the first ship with clothing and foodstuffs from the Soviet Union, arrived in Barcelona at the end of September, two whole months after the outbreak of the revolt.

According to Jean Richard Bloch, October 23rd was the date when the Soviet Union decided upon more effective help, and this probably tallies with the facts. Nevertheless, on November 5th, when the decisive battle of Getafe was raging, no Russian arms were yet to be seen on any of the fronts. In those days we had to defend a seven-kilometre stretch of road between Toledo and Madrid with two old Spanish Hotchkiss machine-guns. Russian military assistance only arrived when the issue had been settled, that is to say, after the International Battalion had repelled the Moorish attack on the University City. I saw our first chasers appear over Villaverde on November 8th. From that date we began to receive arms from Russia—although never in such quantities as were obtained by Franco from Italy and Germany—and then only on those portions of the front where the influence of the Anarchists had been entirely eliminated. In Aragon the first offensive with modern weapons was only begun after the Anarchist Council of Aragon had been dissolved. Before this event, we were without tanks or artillery, and defended ourselves with trench mortars which the Anarchists themselves had manufactured in small village smithies behind the front.

If treason was perpetrated at Malaga, the betrayal was not the work of General Ascencio, who in any case had to be acquitted, but of the Soviet Union, which refused to deliver arms to a province administered by Anarchists. The data will be found in Koestler's *Spanish Testament.* While, therefore, a revolutionary course of events was conceivable from the end of July to the beginning of August 1936, it was no longer to be thought of after the battle of Getafe, which brought the enemy to the suburbs of Madrid. By that time the political and economic difficulties had become insuperable. The P.O.U.M. has been wrongly accused of betrayal. Its only crime was that it endeavoured to force the pace of revolution long after the practical conditions for achieving this object had entirely ceased to obtain. In this connection it must be conceded that after their overwhelming successes in Barcelona, Madrid, Valencia, and Malaga, the revolutionary parties in Spain had begun to take much too rosy a view of their struggle against Fascism. They exclusively took into account the paltry Fascist forces in Spain itself, unmindful of the coming intervention from abroad. At that time, too, it was not so much the people in arms as the parties in arms who were at the front. Officers were chosen for their reliability as party men and not for their military capacities. Each group had its own weapons and stores, and, even during the battle of Getafe, two pieces of light field artillery which were lying in a barn could not be brought into position because they were being kept in reserve by the Anarchists for their own private war. Every party was preparing for the struggle for power after victory had been won.

But when Anarchists and Communists were indiscriminately butchered in Toledo by the Fascists, when the Moors stood before Madrid, the comrades at the front were welded together by the common danger. Foreign intervention wounded Spanish pride, and the new watchword " War for Independence " began to prevail over the idea of social evolution. Such revolutionary slogans as " the Dictatorship of the Proletariat " and " all power to the Councils " became automatically discredited, since nobody wished for the dictatorship of councils or of a party which would be in a position to repress the other groups. The war had to be won and as rapidly as possible ; consequently, everybody wanted unity of command and a strong government. Unfortunately Largo Caballero—that " old skeleton " as Trotsky once called him—was not the man by whose instrumentality these demands could be fulfilled.

This former counsellor of Primo de Rivera was not by any means the Spanish Lenin his partisans had fondly made him out to be. He was only the man on the fence ; deficient in ideas and lacking a guiding principle of his own, he was considered a tolerable choice by Anarchists and Marxists alike. While he was at the helm, he committed as Minister of War almost every mistake of which a statesman is capable. He neglected to fortify the Talavera line at a time when it could have served a useful purpose, he kept the workers of the Madrid building trades busy on the new ministries and the underground railway instead of directing the fortifications of Madrid according to a central plan. He fled from Madrid in excessive haste, without even transferring his authority. He protected and covered incompetent or treacherous generals, and hampered mobilization. He alone was responsible for the long delay in establishing unity of command over the armed forces.

Meanwhile, the Communist party understood better than any other the measures that should be taken to meet the situation. It had a higher percentage of members at the front than any other party ; it also gave an example of discipline when on October 10th it accepted militarization and incorporated its troops in the army. Furthermore, it was responsible for organizing the glorious Fifth

Regiment, the Storm Battalions, and the fortifications of Madrid. Its youth organizations were the driving force in the junta of defence and its Stakhanov workers speeded up production in the industries.

The Communist party counted among its members noble, romantic figures like La Pasionaria, and in Alerta it contrived to create the first type of youth movement that was more than a debating society.

It was also in the happy position of being able to count on international allies. In Paris, at the Cirque d'Hiver, Anarchist ministers were called upon to defend themselves against the charge of participation in the Government ; in Anarchist circles in Holland, it was being debated whether one could still consider as comrades those Spanish Anarchists who had perpetrated the barbarity of defending themselves with firearms against the Fascists. On the other hand, the majority of the volunteers in the international battalions, for whom the word solidarity was a spur to action, were Communists. The first serviceable weapons that came to our hands were of Mexican or Russian origin ; unfortunately, they did not arrive in sufficient quantities. Reports of members of the international brigades are in this respect no indication of the true state of affairs, because the latter were always infinitely better armed, clothed, and fed than the Spanish brigade.

But even in the international brigades there was a pitiable lack of heavy artillery and light machine-guns. Even in October 1937, in the interbrigade training camp at Madrigueras, only seven rifles, one light and one heavy machine-gun were available for two thousand men, and there were no hand-grenades, no ammunition, no barbed wire, no shears, and no Véry lights.

In the case of my own Spanish Communist brigade, we received our first hand-grenades, steel helmets, and gas-masks in April 1937. Uniforms and bayonets arrived in May. In July, our armament still consisted of old English Mausers, of which the barrels burst at the slightest provocation. Among the Anarchist regiments matters were a great deal worse. The seven tanks which were all the Anarchists possessed in the whole of Aragon had been brought over from Mexico and paid for by the organizations themselves.

In Bilbao, delivery of arms from a Russian ship was made conditional upon action being taken against the P.O.U.M., whose influence there was almost non-existent. Our air force consisted of excellent chasers, but we had very few bombers, and the size of our air fleet was always greatly inferior to that of the enemy. It has been reported to me from a reliable source that since December 1936, no more arms have been supplied by Russia, and that the fall of Teruel and what followed had to be imputed to this fact. Certainly, Negrin's speech and the reports in the press seemed to point in the same direction—and, incidentally, cash payments in gold on delivery were the condition for Russian supplies. But the fact that arms at any rate had been supplied by Russia overshadowed all the rest. Undoubtedly, they were of infinitely greater assistance to us than anything that was forthcoming from the Second International and the so-called democratic States. The Second International provided doctors, medicaments, and food ; but the Spaniards who had to surrender a village, where their families were living, because they had run out of hand-grenades, could not help wondering whether the Second International, instead of joining in the common struggle, had not turned itself into a salvation army. The fact that without Russian help we should have been lost—even though this assistance was insufficient to give us victory—naturally aroused tremendous sympathy for Russia among the Spanish youth. Despite the paper shortage the Communist party contrived very cunningly to increase this sympathy by disseminating hundreds of thousands of newspapers, pamphlets, leaflets, films, books, and picture post cards.

The Anarchists allege that the revolution was deliberately obstructed by the Communist party and this allegation is unquestionably correct. The party protected the interests of the small bourgeoisie, and even of speculators; the latter were organized in "trade unions" of bank and stock exchange officials, of dairy producers, meat and fish dealers, of Government officials, etc., and served the party as a counterpoise to the workers in the C.N.T. Syndicates. By introducing the Stakhanov system, the Communists sponsored the principle of a strong differentiation in wages which aroused considerable dissatisfaction among unskilled labour. They refused to consider even such reasonable Anarchist proposals as, for instance, the supervision of the Bourgeois Government and its military courts by organized labour. When militarization was introduced on October 10th, 1936, the discussion of strategic questions was forbidden to the soldiers and since then the significance of the soldiers' meetings has persistently declined. Even political discussion was frowned upon and the army had to be content with mere information imparted by the political commissar. Officers, who until January 1937 were chosen by the men (this was also true in my case), were now appointed and transferred by the Ministry. Originally both militiamen and officers were paid ten pesetas a day, which in proportion to the wages of agricultural labourers was undoubtedly too high. At a later date, two and a half pesetas were kept back for food and clothing, while henceforth the militiamen had also to pay for their own stamps, tobacco, tram fares, and other small disbursements. At the same time, however, officers were given a tremendous rise ; a lieutenant at the front was paid 220 pesetas, a captain 350 pesetas for the ten days. A graver departure was the setting up of officers' clubs, especially among Communist units, to which the men had no access, and the introduction of a special officers' kitchen even at the front. When this innovation was rejected at an officers' gathering of my battalion because, as Sentella put it, they did not wish the soldiers in the trenches to begrudge us our food, a political commissar set out from Madrid to convince us that our objection was a " Left " deviation. The soldiers would have to get used to the fact that after victory we should be living in a democratic republic and not in anarchist equality. At the same time as the introduction of the new uniforms, which had to bc kept fastened at the neck even in the greatest heat, the compulsory salute and heavy disciplinary punishments made their first appearance. The German-speaking Eleventh Brigade was in all these matters singled out to us as an example, particularly after Richard had managed to get rid of Renn as chief-of-staff. Our training camp at Madrigueras was under the command of Heinz, a fine person, a brave soldier, a convinced Communist, and an indefatigable worker. Training was excellent and discipline exemplary. Unfortunately Heinz had taken the old Prussian army as his model. In this respect, like most German officers, he seemed to lack all understanding of the mentality of Spaniards, or for that matter of the Dutchmen and Scandinavians who had been incorporated in this brigade.

At an officers' gathering a Spanish captain was raising objections to the compulsory salute, which compelled us to go about the streets of a small place like Madrigueras with our fist perpetually raised to our hat. " Comrade," replied a German lieutenant, " take to heart the words of an old revolutionary : if in Spain you had had from the very beginning the discipline of our Red Front league, the Fascists would never have reached Madrid ! " At another gathering I was given to understand that mine was the best company of the whole battalion, but that it was unpleasant for the officers of other companies that so few punishments were meted out. Even in sexual matters the new puritanism of the Soviet Union was imitated. Wherever the International Brigades were garrisoned, the brothels were closed and the word was passed on by the Communists that " venereal disease is desertion." Our political commissar, who was a Communist, averred that a

Communist should be able to control his sexual impulses. Unfortunately our men were far from being all Communists, and their sexual starvation during months spent at the front without ever seeing a woman was very damaging to their morale.

Anarchist newspapers never reached the trenches : they were kept back by the political commissars, who were Communists in the majority. But in any event, it would be difficult to blame them for this action. The spiteful and venomous tone of these papers, which seemed to be directed a great deal more against the Government and the Marxists than against the enemy, was anything but conducive to improving the morale of the troops. Consequently, the Anarchists saw their influence dwindle in many sectors of the front, while behind the front the U.G.T. in particular managed to draw unto itself groups of the lower middle classes which so far had been non-political. Membership of the Anarchist groups fell off proportionately as that of the Marxist groups increased. Thrust out of the Government, the Anarchists were inclined to take the view that this Government's victory might signify the complete loss of their own influence and their future liquidation by the Communists. Furthermore, the framework in which Russian society had been moulded was as unattractive to them as that of Fascism. While dreading defeat they had no further interest in a victory at any rate of this Government, with the result that they marked time and thereby paralysed the building up of a war industry in Catalonia, the most important industrial centre.

To maintain their membership up to scratch, they gave admittance without sufficient previous investigation to a number of elements which often were keen upon obtaining a membership card of the C.N.T., primarily as a protection against the secret police. In view of the semi-illegal condition in which the P.O.U.M. had to work, it was naturally even more easy for agents provocateurs and spies, equipped with the necessary radical phraseology, to enter there. Endeavours were then made to bind the members by exacting labour conditions and wages which could only result in a rapid rise in prices ; inferior workers were protected, and, furthermore, food convoys and cars were commandeered and placed at the disposal of friends. It was not surprising that in the end this intolerable state of affairs in Catalonia had to be fought to a finish. On the subject of the main causes that brought the conflict to a head, history will say that right was on the side of the Government. It became as necessary to replace the Anarchist frontier posts by the newly organized carabineros, as it was to abolish the voluntary police corps of the various parties, and it was intolerable that the Barcelona central telephone office, which might have to be made use of at any moment by military headquarters, was supervised and guarded by armed trade unionists. It is equally true, however, that the manner in which the central telephone office was occupied by the police inevitably had the effect of a provocation. It should be added that the Communist chief of police who was responsible for the order was subsequently dismissed.

On the other hand, it is not correct, in my view, that the conflict in Barcelona was deliberately provoked by the P.O.U.M. It should be remembered that the P.O.U.M. never was a Trotskyist party, but a combination of three of the older Marxist parties in the B.O.G. (the peasant and workers bloc), which Trotsky had openly trounced for being established on a too democratic basis and for its naughtiness in refusing to have anything to do with the Fourth International. Nor is it any more in accordance with the facts that the conflict in Barcelona ended in a complete victory for the Government troops. The end was brought about through the good offices of the Anarchist leaders who had come over from Valencia.

It is a fact, however, that throughout the country, and especially in the army, the conflict in Barcelona was grist to the Communist mill. Nobody who was in the trenches in those days is likely to forget this stab in the back. The general view was that perhaps there had been provocation, but that nobody should allow himself to be provoked to such lengths. The conflict in Barcelona constituted an annihilating blow to the political influence of the Anarchists.

After the events in Barcelona, it was generally considered that henceforth the Government would fall entirely under the influence of the Communists. I noted, however—and the fact was corroborated by the *Temps* of January 11th, 1938—that the very reverse took place. These events were interpreted by the Government as a warning not to proceed too far against organizations which still included millions of Spaniards. It realized the danger of a coalition of these elements with the Catalan autonomists, who were active and very distrusted at the time. The split in the U.G.T. and the Caballero episode, although of greater personal than political significance, incited the Government to caution. Its removal to Barcelona resulted not only in repressing all autonomist tendencies and in finally helping to put the Catalan war industry on its feet, but it also and primarily brought a considerable *détente* in the political situation. Nor did the Government, after the Anarchist State within the State had been broken, hesitate to defend its independence also against the Communists.

The International Brigade was the stronghold of the Communist party ; almost all the officers and political commissars were Communists. The first step, therefore, was to subordinate completely the Interbrigade and its services to the Spanish supreme command, and to appoint Spanish officers in proportion to the number of Spanish soldiers (60 per cent.) ; the next move was to purge the cadre bureaus and the staff and deprive them of all party political activity. The removal of Alvarez del Vayo, as general commissar for the army, and the replacement of 250 Communist political commissars of the Brigade by others constituted a final very important step in this direction. It will be asked how an independent policy of this nature was possible in view of the Government's dependence upon Russia for the supply of arms. In the first place it was considered that these deliveries would gradually become less important in proportion as Catalonia was developing its own war industry. In the second place this dependence was not without its dangers for the Spanish people themselves.

From the very beginning Russia's attitude had never been as plain and transparent as, for instance, that of Mexico. Despite its fervent declarations at Geneva in favour of Spain, Russia adhered with a bleeding heart to the fatal policy of non-intervention for the sake of its friendship with France. Although on October 23rd the Soviet Union resumed its liberty of action, its attitude was so rigidly legalistic that, in the case of a revolution in Portugal, it absolutely refused all assistance to those who might rise up against their "legal" dictatorial government. Maisky spoke hard and true words in London, but in the end the ultimatum to Italy remained a dead letter. There is no reason to assume that Italian Fiats were run on Russian oil; nevertheless it always seems easier for Soviet aeroplanes to fly to America by the North Pole than from Kiev to Barcelona. Even at Teruel the number of government aeroplanes was inferior to that of the enemy. In the negotiations for the recall of the volunteers and the recognition of belligerent rights to Franco, Maisky has until now given way to England step by step. That this should be so is not surprising. The endless series of executions in the Soviet Union do not testify to great internal stability; the army has been robbed of its most brilliant leaders, while with every day the danger of war increases.

Chiang Kai-Shek, who as recently as 1927 allowed 11,000 Communists to be murdered in Shanghai alone, is not a particularly reliable ally, and the army of the Chinese Soviet Republics is being used up on the various fronts. If Chiang Kai-Shek should again, as in the days of Borodin, commit an act of betrayal and make his peace with Japan, this country would be able to make use of China's four hundred millions against the Soviet Union. In these circumstances Russia could not expose itself to the hostility of England, and in proportion as the shoe pinched in the East, was constrained to agree to more and more concessions to England in the matter of Spain. The Spanish Republic had every reason for being sceptical of Mr. Eden, of Franco's financial backers in the City, and of British large scale capitalists with shares in Rio Tinto. It took the only right view, that the Spanish people must free itself.

Since these lines were written, events in Spain have taken an increasingly dramatic and tragic course.

Last November I was still full of hope and confidence in the building up of the Spanish army which the Negrin Government had taken in hand with exemplary energy. At last the training colleges were turning out excellent officers; the instruction and the spirit of the soldiers were first rate; we had enormous reserves of man power at our disposal, whereas Franco was unable to call upon any more from his own territory. A great cry of misery rose up from the Fascist correspondence seized at Brunete, while the number of deserters who came over to us continually increased, and all they said pointed to growing despair and bitterness in " National Spain."

Books such as *Doy Fe*, *Yo He Creido en Franco*, the expulsion of the Duke of Parma (the Carlist Pretender) and the departure of the Jesuits, everything suggested that tension was increasing between Spaniards and foreigners on Franco's side. In *Aftonposton*, Gissholdt, the Norwegian Franco volunteer published three long articles, describing the rapid disintegration of the forces both in the military and economic field. True, we had lost on the isolated battle front of the Asturias, but this Pyrrhic victory cost Franco more dead than the total of our forces in those northern fastnesses ; it cost him the reserves which were required to attack the central front. Franco's requests for help to Mussolini became more urgent every day. Mussolini, however, refused to send fresh troops so long as Germany was not further committed. Meanwhile on the central front we were marching from victory to victory at Brunete, Belchite, and Quinto. It was therefore no miracle that Teruel fell to us ; it was the crown and consummation of an effort systematically pursued. With the recall of even Conservative deputies and the summoning of the Cortes, it looked as if the Government had a good chance of regaining the confidence of the so-called democracies.

The fall of Teruel and the failure of Franco's

offensives, however, spelt for Mussolini a loss of prestige and position which could not possibly be borne by the weak Italian dictatorship. A final call for help went out to Hitler, and Hitler saw his chance of realizing the dream of his life.

The generals were against further intervention : they distrusted their Italian allies, they feared a war that could no longer be a lightning knock-out blow, and in their view the inclusion of Spain meant a dangerous extension of the front.

The generals were set aside.

Franco received, apart from Italian infantry, the overwhelming air force and tank material that was necessary to him—while Hitler was made a present of Austria.

In England, Mr. Eden, who was ready to sell the Spanish Republic for Italian guarantees, was replaced by Lord Halifax, who was ready to do so even without these guarantees.

With a humanitarian protest against the frightful bombardments of Barcelona, Pontius Pilate Chamberlain washed his hands in innocency, and the Second International—including its revered member, Leon Blum, who had non-intervention upon his conscience—discovered the mistake of non-intervention when Caspe had already fallen.

In France, the Popular Front which was to protect us against Fascism was nowhere to be found, and when the French General Staff, but not the French working-class movement, thought of intervention at the eleventh hour, it lacked the support of its only ally, Russia, which had decapitated itself with its own trials.

Those whom the gods would destroy they first strike with blindness. The working-classes in Europe have deserved their fate, but not the peasants and workers of Spain who have fought with unparalleled courage not only for their liberties but for our own. They are now perishing from our cowardice. Theirs is a tragedy exceeding in majesty that of any of the Greek dramatic poets.

Is there no bright spot in this tragedy?

Again the Spanish militiamen with their unconquerable heroism have held up the advance and thwarted all the plans of Mussolini and Lord Halifax. The new Spanish Government—which also includes Anarchists, while the Communists with one exception have withdrawn—represents the Spanish people far more closely than its predecessor. The reinstatement of the P.O.U.M. as well as the fusion which has finally come about between the C.N.T. and the U.G.T. constitute a big step forward. The Daladier Government is showing more backbone with regard to Spain than the Government of the Popular Front, and Russia, feeling itself no longer bound by the Popular Front, has resumed its deliveries of arms on a modest scale. In Geneva, the promises solemnly made to Alvarez del Vayo on behalf of the Republic have once more been repudiated, but the United States is contemplating the raising of the embargo on arms for Spain. Franco is again at the end of his tether, his reserves are exhausted, while Mussolini, for whom Spain overshadows all other questions, is using the so-called new deliveries to the Republic as a pretext for resuming his intervention on a still larger scale. All things are still possible : Italian neutrality may be bought by sacrificing the Republic, or a breach may be effected in the Anglo-Franco-Italian negotiations which have been initiated. However grim the outlook, there always remains the bright hope of the youth of Spain, which will inevitably rise up again as soon as the last Italian or German soldier has been withdrawn from the country, as soon as the terrible losses endured by the wholesale massacre of the best have been more or less made up. And there yet remains another hope : from all their terrible defeats the proletariat may now have learnt their lesson.

But can this lesson be learnt in the hey-day of a period which has evolved a technique of systematic lying, vilification, and distrust ? Is it still possible at a time when all reason, understanding, and honesty are shouted down by party fanaticism, party blindness, and party hatred ; at a time when force, which is worshipped also on our side, is ready to crush anybody who wishes to think independently, and not in accordance with party lines ? It would seem as if we had forsaken God and set up in His place our new and all-devouring idols, the race, the State, the party, the organization. It would seem as if we had all become like Don Quixote, who never cared for a being of flesh and blood, and who therefore went about smashing heads in the name of his ideals.

So it would appear. And yet in all parties, in all groups, there is a force which is hated and feared, which is annihilated only to be resuscitated, and springs from the very salt of the earth, the force of holy opposition.

Only the path of systematic questioning leads to knowledge. Only by discussion are we spurred on to think out our thoughts to their ultimate conclusions and to make them our very own.

Character is only developed through conflict. A new Soviet constitution should guarantee to all the right to love, to acquire a sense of responsibility, to think freely, to doubt, even to err.

May we then be permitted to doubt that salvation lies only in armed opposition and to question whether the working-classes have not other, more effective, weapons in their possession. There is something to be learnt even from Gandhi ; not everything, but certainly rather more than is imagined by the dogmatists of Marx. Let us no longer consider the State as an ideal, but merely as the framework in which the people have their being, as the dead shell, the trappings of the living and evolving organism.

Organization has been idolized. Let us now see the other side and consider whether the absence of organization is not at least as strong a weapon in the armoury of the working-classes. Organization is indispensable to the processes of building up. But revolution broke out not in countries with powerful and wealthy organizations, but in Russia and Spain, where a soulless organization was weakest but where the living party, in other words, spiritual unity, was strongest.

In these days of finger-prints, radio, and Gestapo, organization often amounts to not much more than making out the lists for the concentration camps. Co-operative undertakings, party funds, party headquarters, whatever constituted strength, may under the inspiration of fear become so many obstacles to action, until the moment arrives when this rich booty falls into the hands of the enemy. Organized opposition has spelt defeat again and again at the hands of an incomparably better organized and equipped opponent. And yet a thousand resolute men, each acting on his own, could bring about the collapse of a régime—if such men were to be found.

But men hanker after their lost childhood ; they are prepared to be only the children of God, of Hitler, or of Stalin, so long as they are not required to think and father defends them against the bad boys. It follows that organization is only too often the magical word that absolves one from independent thinking, from assuming responsibilities. Organization means only too often waiting " without allowing oneself to be provoked " for the " word of command," which never comes because meanwhile the leaders have been decapitated, or perhaps only seduced . . .

The writer is no quack doctor prescribing pills for curing a patient at the eleventh hour. He is not even a believer in a war of the " Democracies " against the " Fascist States." He is convinced that within a few weeks of such a war the " Democratic Countries " would go Fascist under a " National Cabinet," while with their lives the flower of the working-class would foot the bill for the arms manufacturers. In so far as he still believes in war after an experience of thirteen months, he believes with Lenin that the enemy is always within one's own gate, and that only a revolutionary war can bring salvation to the proletariat. He is interested in the destruction of Fascism in Germany, but has no interest in a new Versailles or in the partitioning of Germany, where the revolution would be stifled by the military forces of the invader. He is, however, too much of a realist to believe in the possibility of a revolutionary war for a long time to come.

The road to Socialism is long and arduous ; it is the road leading to man's fuller humanity. To achieve this end, co-operation is necessary, and not merely in an organization. There must be co-operation in spirit, in the good and loyal comradeship of all who, whatsoever their party or political inclinations, are sick to death of the whole swindle, and are ready solely on their own responsibility to stake their very lives for the future of humanity.

FOREIGNERS

Madrid, October 10th, 1936.

A FEW DAYS BEFORE WE LEFT, I READ IN *REX voor Vlaanderen*, a Flemish sheet, the following headline : " Without French help Irun would already be Spanish ! "

The words were completely in keeping with the now prevalent habit of describing the rebels as the " National Troops," whereas the lawfully constituted army of the Republic comes under the general title of " the Reds."

Let us endeavour to consider the position objectively.

" National Troops " are the officers who took the oath to the Republic, and drew their pay from the Republic, only that they might conspire in secret against this Republic.

" National Troops " are they who, with the support of Italian and German machines, bombed Spanish towns and villages, and they who on Portuguese territory concluded agreements for the delivery of war material to be paid for later on with Spanish islands and Moroccan aerodromes.

" National troops " include the Moorish mercenaries who were pressed into service with promises of plunder from Spanish cities. They include the foreign legion, that refuge of the dregs of humanity, where without questions as to name and origin everybody gains admission who is prepared for money to shoot at anybody upon his officer's instructions.

The " Reds," on the other hand, are the workers of Madrid, who voluntarily took up arms in their tens of thousands, the peasants of Castile, the Asturian miners, the simple village priests of the Basque Country, the painters and intellectuals of the capital, Bergamin, leader of the Catholic youth, and the Nationalists of Catalonia.

The emaciated women who flew to arms ; the sixteen-year-old boy who reported for duty this morning, fourth son of a household where three brothers are already at the front ; the militiaman in the trench whose bushy eyebrows were half obliterated in the downpour of rain ; the agricultural labourer who smilingly showed us his papers, marked with the royal stamp which proclaimed him unfit for service ; the student of architecture, who harnessed like a horse was dragging up the guns ; the professor of mathematics who was the student's battery commandant—all these are the " Reds." And there are also foreigners in the Republican army, for am I not a foreigner ?

The struggle in Spain is not only a struggle for the democratic Republic ; it is a struggle for democracy in Europe.

Peace is indivisible and international solidarity is a condition for the maintenance of peace ; hence anti-fascists from every country hurried to the rescue.

The defeat of democracy in Spain means in strategical terms that the ring around France is closed and that Fascism can begin a world war with the greatest possible assurance of victory.

Like peace itself, the cause of the world proletariat is one and indivisible, and the word " international " would cease to have meaning if proletarians of every country had not of their own accord rushed to succour their comrades in Spain.

I know dozens of German refugees who, after collecting their last pennies from relief funds, travelled to Paris in order to offer their services as volunteers. But I know, too, that almost all of them were rejected, because the Spanish Republic had an abundance of volunteers and was short of weapons. As a general rule, only those were enrolled who for military or other reasons were of special value for war operations.

It is a known fact that in the North the strategic defence was mainly directed by a French captain of the reserve and a German refugee who had gone through the Great War. The French captain was killed defending the last earthwork, and we do not know his name.

The German was called Hoffman. According to a friend who was watching operations from the French frontier, Hoffman was holding the line against the Foreign Legion. During the night, whenever rifle fire subsided for a moment, Hoffman was heard to call out : " Kameraden ! Ihr seid Proleten wie wir ! Warum kämpft ihr nicht mit uns gegen eure Unterdrücker ? " (Comrades, we are all proletarians together ! Why don't you fight with us against your oppressors ?)

Whenever he called out volley firing followed almost immediately. Shortly before dawn the bullets hit their mark, and Hoffman's voice was stilled. But his words were taken up by the anti-fascist combatants, and will continue to resound in the ears of the " National troops " : " Comrades, why don't you fight with us against your oppressors ? "

Yes, these two were foreigners bent upon serving the cause of Spanish democracy. There is also the old Austrian, whose acquaintance I made on my first evening in Madrid in the central barracks of the Fifth Regiment. He was taken prisoner in the world war by the Russians, and then fought shoulder to shoulder with his former foes against Koltchak in Siberia. He was a metal worker in Vienna until Dolfuss's *coup d'état.* His wife and only boy were killed during the bombardment of the workmen's flats in Vienna. Here in barracks he is among the few who know how to handle a machine-gun. I have also come across two students from Oxford, who happened to be spending their holiday in Spain when the revolt broke out. Both were pacifists : "That was why we joined up," they said.

They too are foreigners ; they constitute perhaps one in every ten thousand, scattered up and down the divisions defending the fronts, in the South, the Centre, the West and the East. It is seldom they meet and then by the merest accident, but their presence in Spain is proof enough that solidarity is not a vain and empty word.

They are foreigners ; but the Spanish comrades do all they can to make them forget that they are aliens. To say that every comrade in barracks is for them a friend and every mate a brother is an understatement. The Spaniards are proud of the foreigners in their midst, as one might be proud of a new and very unusual banner. They take them round the terrifying working-class districts of Madrid which are perhaps the most poverty-stricken slums in the world. They show them off to their acquaintances. They invite them to their homes for a meal and apologize for the meagreness of the fare. Women stop them in the streets and from their poverty provide them with melons and figs. Children hang upon their arm. Grey-bearded workers embrace them. These foreign volunteers are overloaded with articles of clothing from the quartermaster's stores; not a single militiaman sets out for the front so well equipped. When food fails to arrive in the firing line they are given the last soaked hunk of bread that is left over in the quartermaster-sergeant's bag.

Foreigners they may be, but nowhere have I seen such spontaneous cordiality as here exists between comrades who barely understand one another, and I catch myself repeating the words that one of them addressed to me very slowly and almost mockingly, as if to imprint them well upon my mind: "Todos los proletarios del mundo son hermanos!" (All the proletarians of the world are brothers.)

October 12th.

We were about twenty men all told, sent out to fill up the gaps in a company that had been out at the front for two months. Shortly before leaving, a comrade invited me to come and partake of the midday meal at his house. He was a skilled metal-worker and had a rather nice little home. While his wife was preparing food he took me round his vegetable garden. The potato and tomato beds were dried up and neglected. " Perdido ! " This was the third time he was going to the front ; there was nobody to look after the garden in his absence. A five-year-old little girl and a tiny rascal of three were clinging to their father and clambering on his knees during the meal. His wife waited upon us, her eyes red with crying. But when we said good-bye, her last words were : " No pasaran ! " (They won't break through !) And from the road we could still see her standing at the veranda with her clenched fist raised.

" Our Spanish women have gone through a lot," my friend said with sudden gravity. " But what is one to do ? There is no other road to freedom ! "

As we were marching to the station the comrades were singing the International, the Young Guard, and the Red Flag. Everybody was in good spirits, but nobody was drunk or boisterous. Among them I saw Nicasio, who is seventeen, and Orubio, a farm-hand from the mountains, who had a three days' journey on foot before joining up with us. During our first days in barracks, Orubio afforded us much amusement : with his razor he had cut out a sickle and hammer in his close-cropped hair. Such a notion could only occur to a village youth. One afternoon while I was walking down the Avenida de la Republica beside Orubio, he suddenly burst into sobs without apparent reason. He pointed to a woman who was suckling a baby while a small girl of about two years old was hanging on to her skirts. " Mine were just that age," he said, " when the Fascists shot them down together with my wife, just because she would not tell them where I was hiding."

From that moment it was no longer possible to laugh at Orubio's sickle and hammer. He himself explained it in this way : " If the Fascists should happen to catch me they will at any rate know I am a Communist."

At the Atocha station the empty restaurant and sleeping-cars of the international trains had been side-tracked. Under the enormous roof only one puffing little train was standing ready to take us to the front. The second-class carriages were reserved for the military. Our comrades got in and took their seats rather primly, as they might have sat down on easy chairs in a very respectable home. Neither a scratch on the wood nor a stain on the velvet upholstery was to be seen.

In the carriage adjoining ours a lieutenant-colonel was sitting next to his soldiers ; he was still wearing the uniform of the old regular army. I went and sat beside him and began to converse with him in French. " When the revolution broke out," he said, " we were given the choice between taking the oath to the Republic and retiring from the service on full pay. Franco took the oath in order to make doubly sure that the war material of the Republic would fall completely into his hands. For me, however, an oath is an oath and a traitor a traitor. In Toledo Mola got his Moors to despatch 700 of our militiamen—700 prisoners." He pointed to the comrades around us in the carriage : " 700 boys like these, the best human material Spain ever had. And these people call themselves Nationalists ! " It was now dark in the compartment. As we entered the actual war zone the train proceeded with lights extinguished. Naval Perral was the last post still occupied by our troops. While behind the range of hills machine-guns were angrily rattling, we were taken in the dark to a country house that had been commandeered. We wrapped ourselves up in our blankets and slept as best we could, our heads resting on our rucksacks.

Our positions consist of grey boulders, linked up here and there by breastworks of carelessly piled up stones. Behind us in the valley lies Naval Perral, where shells are constantly exploding in a whirling mass of dust and stone. In front of us, along the upper mountain ridge that enfolds the village, the Moors are holding the line, invisible behind their boulders. Twice already the village has fallen into their hands and twice the Mangada column has captured it from the enemy. They are now endeavouring for the third time to close the iron ring around us, which now has only a narrow exit in the direction of Navas del Marques, where the armoured train unceasingly travels up and down the line. Meanwhile the circle has become so narrow that the plateau we are occupying is swept not only by the enemy opposite us, but also by the more haphazard bullets right and left on our flanks.

Although we have been stationed here three days and three nights, there is still not a single heroic deed to report of our company. After Sunday's big bombardment, when the enemy hurled more than two thousand shells on our village, it was generally assumed that an attack of Moorish cavalry was impending. With nerves on edge we peered out into the darkness. There was whispering among the comrades : "Remember not to use up your last bullet. If we are captured by the Moors we shall not just be shot, they will cut us up alive with their bayonets." Our cartridge cases lay open, and our hands were on the bolt, but there was no attack. The rumour went round that the Moors, disheartened by the cold, had refused to attack. Later on in the night, on other sectors of the front, machine-guns began to bark again like dogs suddenly gone mad, but over our heads only a few stray bullets came buzzing by now and then like vicious wasps or buried themselves with a thud in the stones of the breastwork. Our real foes were not enemy bullets but the cold and the rain. Throughout that first night the downpour was unceasing. Gradually the suspense was eased, and when only the sentries were on the watch, we lay huddled together swathed in our blankets and shivering on the gleaming wet stones. Thus dawn broke upon us while more inky grey masses of cloud slowly approached from behind the mountains of the West. Ice-cold mists trailed over us, enveloping us again and again for minutes at a time. There was not a ray of sun all day. By this time our shoes and socks were drenched, and our blankets were weighing like lead upon our shoulders. There was no warm food to be got because a few enemy shells had landed in the middle of our kitchen utensils. The second day our line of communications with the village was swept by the enemy's artillery and we found ourselves even without bread, sausage, and wine. This morning our sergeant crept on his belly through the line of fire and came back with a small cask of wine and a few bunches of grapes. Each of us only received half a glass, for—as the men put it—" if you drink too much on an empty stomach you can no longer shoot straight." Although the bullets were flying closer than yesterday over our heads, little Nicasio was moving backwards and forwards on the level ground, cutting thistles with his bayonet. We lit a miserable fire behind the biggest boulder which gave more smoke than heat.

At eleven o'clock the captain came along : " We must contrive to hold out somehow till five o'clock," he said. " All the reserves are necessary for the other sectors, where the enemy is attacking all the time. I can only relieve those who feel positively ill."

Nobody reported himself sick.

In our blankets, drenched through and through, we squatted behind the rocks, and Jesus Martin Perez, a street scavenger from Madrid, who was lying beside me was saying : " That's not so bad—

to be relieved at five o'clock. A fortnight ago we had to lie for eight days on end among the rocks, and for three days with no food at all."

I feel it cannot be sufficiently stressed that without a single exception all our militiamen are volunteers, and our regiments are nothing but armed party groups. From October 10th, however, militarization has been introduced as well as unity of command under the Ministry of War; at the same time a new form of military discipline, severe though democratic, has come into force. Firmly convinced of the people's will to win, the Government in the middle of the war have left it optional to all who do not approve of militarization to be released of their obligation to serve and to go home on October 10th.

That afternoon we were relieved by a company which had arrived from Madrid a few hours before. Nearly all were volunteers who were at the front for the first time. Not only in years but in their whole deportment they were like children still. They took over our rifles, and they were singing as we saw them disappear one by one behind the ridge. Clearly, the words "Sabemos vencer o morir" (We know how to conquer or die), from the "Young Guard," were to them much more than an empty slogan.

Without weapons we were kept in our villa as a

reserve. Throughout the next day we were able to follow the operations from the room in the turret. The enemy launched a desperate offensive, and, for the space of a few hours, was successful in cutting off the only road that connected us with Madrid. Our Captain alone had a revolver. Grimly the boys were saying : " If they now break through, the Moors will catch us alive after all ! " From the North another air-attack was reported.

At that moment the sergeants came to announce that our political delegate would address us on the meaning of militarization in the large hall downstairs. Five minutes later we had forgotten all about the Moors and the aeroplanes over our heads. Discussion raged with passionate intensity. There were farm hands who could not understand the difference between a capitalist and a democratic discipline. They were saying, " We were soldiers under the King, and if we now fight as volunteers, it is so that our children should never become soldiers." And others declared : " They can order us a dozen times if they like ; we shall still refuse to shoot our comrades for some piece of stupidity or other."

The objections of the Anarchists were deeper and more fundamental. As one of them put it : " We are the people in arms, the fighters of the revolution, and we refuse to be degraded to the level of troops of a bourgeois government, with no will of our own."

Our delegate reminded them that even the Syndicalists had stressed in their newspapers the necessity for an iron discipline. He said that the co-operation and supervision of the parties offered a guarantee that the troops could not possibly be misused. He pointed out that so far our losses had been ten times as great as they would have been if military discipline and proper drill had been enforced. He emphasized the all-importance of victory, and that victory against the militarily trained forces of the rebels could only be achieved by rigidly submitting to a single military leadership.

Without reaching a definite decision the gathering dispersed. The electric light had been cut off and everywhere in the rooms and passages the shutters were closed. We groped back in the dark and settled ourselves down on the floor to snatch some sleep. Rifle-fire had diminished and we heard that our troops had recaptured their old positions.

Three days later our company returned on leave to Madrid. Those who were in agreement with militarization were instructed to report two days later at their barracks. This morning in the courtyard I saw that they had all come back—Orubio, José, Nicasio, and our Jesus, who was the spokesman of the Anarchists. One by one they were given their new pay-book. Jesus greeted me by encircling my wrist with his hand after the fashion of the Anarchists. He smiled, as he gave me to understand that we were all one company and should stick together ; the main point was to conquer !

It now looks as if in two days' time we shall again set out for the front with these same " bandits." It is reported that snow is already lying on the Sierra.

BEHIND THE FRONT

October 20th.

MADRID HAS CHANGED. I KNEW THE GRAN VIA and the Calle de Alcala with their ostentatious skyscrapers and ostentatious display of luxury cars ; the blasé snobbery of the international hotels ; the aimless sauntering along the boulevards ; the cafés where, above the endless conversations, time itself stood still in a blue mist of cigarette smoke. I had known the crocks, the beggars, the mothers exploiting the misery of their children in the underground, at the entrance of banks, hotels, and theatres, in the parks, and on the steps of churches. I was acquainted with the dark recesses of the slum quarters, and the gleaming cocked hats of the civil guard, which put one in mind of lacquered coffins.

The beggars have disappeared at the same time as the civil guard ; the luxury cars have been commandeered and are crudely daubed over with white or red lettering. The bored and lounging bourgeoisie have been swept off the streets, to be replaced by a teeming crowd in uniform, or rather—for it is impossible to talk of uniforms here—the streets are overflowing with workers in overalls, who are recognizable as militiamen by their forage cap and belt, by a revolver or a rifle slung round their shoulder. They give the town its new tone and appearance : the unmistakable proletarian visage of the revolution.

No, I have not seen a single broken window-pane anywhere, neither in the centre of the town nor in the working-class districts. All the shops are open ; the cheap stores as well as the jewellers ; the large luxury establishments as well as the food and provision shops. Everything is still obtainable and we find that prices are lower than in Paris. The police, even those on point duty, have disappeared from the city. A remarkable fact is the sudden and almost complete disappearance of crime. On all hands we have been assured that no robberies occur in Madrid. Up to a point this is comprehensible : the proletariat have a thousand eyes where the police have only two. Robbery in these days is robbery of the people, and the people mete out punishment with ruthless severity.

A militiaman in our barracks, who was caught red-handed stealing a purse, was condemned to death by his own comrades and shot an hour later.

In one of the Castilian villages the whole revolutionary committee were executed because they had personally enriched themselves in the process of commandeering Fascist property.

The spirit of the people is best expressed in the words of my alvarez (second lieutenant), when he said to me, " For us the position is perfectly simple. It is not only a question of ' Conquering or dying ' ; if we die, all hope dies with us, all progress, all that makes life worth living. Everything that represents the arts, the intellect, humanism, is on our side. On the other side are ranged the most overbearing and stupid middle class, the most insolent landowners, and most ignorant ecclesiastics the world has ever known. It follows that the struggle can never come to an end, so long as there remain ten people alive who really care for Spain. Opposition will flare up again and again . . ."

But—I can hear you say—what about the Church ? Can it be denied that religion and its servants have been persecuted in the most frightful manner, that the blood of the priests has again been flowing, as in the days of the first Christian martyrs ?

Let us tread warily. The clergy are living in glass houses and the church of Spain, that can look back upon *auto-dafés* and the inquisition, has little reason for recoiling from blood. Free thought has its martyrs too, and the name of Ferrer is still remembered. Priests have been struck down, but many were bearing the cross in one hand and wielding a revolver in the other. Churches have been blown up, but their towers were nests of machine-guns ; monasteries were set on fire, but behind their walls Moorish sharp-shooters were lurking with their rifles !

The 'planes that bomb the working-class districts and schools of Madrid are decorated with the blessed image of St. Christopher, and an enamelled model of the Sacred Heart of Jesus is to be found on every one of Franco's tanks. To say this is not to deny that everywhere, except in the Basque country, the churches are closed—even in the smallest villages—that the priests have been driven away or killed ; that the monks and nuns are in flight. While these facts are not denied, we say that the church itself, and not the revolutionary nation, has to defend itself against the most fearful indictment ever drawn up by history.

From Moorish times thc Catholic Church has reigned unchallenged in Spain over twenty-five million souls. The Moors and Jews were expelled and the heretics burnt. Government, education, works of mercy, the press, the arts, and the censorship were in its hands. From the day of his birth to the day of his death, every citizen of Spain fell under its influence. Its wealth was untold and its ecclesiastics more numerous than in any other country of the world.

But now, after more than ten centuries of official Catholicism, the people have drawn up the balance sheet : it would seem that the priesthood, for all their unceasing endeavour, have only succeeded in sowing in the hearts of millions of industrial workers and peasants an angry contempt and loathing for a church which throughout these centuries has deliberately allied itself to exploitation and oppression.

Every day these people set out voluntarily for the battlefields in their tens of thousands. Without exception they have been baptized and confirmed ; many have been married in the church and all have heard the priest in the pulpit preach on the subject of hell and purgatory.

But of all these ten thousands not one is afraid of eternal damnation, not one seems to want the last sacraments at the hands of a priest when his last hour arrives. I have seen them die on the battlefields, and their eyes have put me in mind of trampled flowers.

Even the enemy has recognized the heroism of these free thinkers in the face of death. Can there be a greater indictment of the Church of Spain than the fact that hundreds of thousands of its sons reject its last sacraments in the full consciousness that death is staring them in the face ?

I see in front of me the highly strung, spiritual figure of Bergamin, the well-known catholic philosopher and writer. His movements have a certain stiffness, a woodenness that suggests an invalid. In actual fact he is a perpetual source of energy and inspiration. " Bergamin," said Alberti, " is the bravest of us all."

I have been talking to Bergamin in one of the small restaurants of Madrid : sitting opposite me is one who is crying in the wilderness, and listening, listening hard for an answering call from a brother somewhere behind the horizon.

" I know," Bergamin is saying, " that the social renaissance of catholicism is just as necessary as the spiritualization of a communism which left to itself must inevitably sink in the slough of opportunism. I know that communion and communism have the same root, and that, in despite of all reason, our hearts have already drawn together because we all wish for righteousness on behalf of those who are nearest to Christ, the humble of this earth. It is no pure accident that the Apostles of Christ were labourers and not generals like Mola ! "

BERGAMIN, CATHOLIC AND REVOLUTIONARY

UPON MEETING HIM FOR THE FIRST TIME, MY MIND went back to one of Greco's canvases : it was only there I could have seen a face so instinct with spirituality. Unconsciously I was tempted to look for some physical defect—only to discover later on the magnificent masculine vitality of this seemingly so fragile figure. From the very first moment you sense Bergamin's spiritual superiority to all who surround him, but the warm humanity he exudes is so intense that all feeling of inferiority is banished in advance. In his company you feel as if somebody of the nature of Francis of Assisi had suddenly assumed flesh and blood.

Bergamin is the son of one of the best-known lawyers of Madrid who was also Conservative minister under the monarchy. He himself was a student of law. " But that was a mistake," his friends will tell you with a smile ; " throughout his life Bergamin has been interested not in the law but in justice." This feeling for justice is with him indissolubly bound up with his profoundly Catholic conception of life.

He is now sitting opposite me at this little café table, the man who upon being consulted as a Catholic by the Government declared *against* the reopening of the churches in Madrid. " Rather the catacombs ! That at least would be genuine and true. The problem of Catholicism goes too deep for us to be satisfied with a purely opportunist solution for the sake of propaganda abroad. The question of opening or closing churches is irrelevant. The point at issue is the revival of a true and pure Catholicism in the hearts of men."

Such words could only be spoken by the man who three years ago, in the very title of his periodical, laid down the programme which was to be a clarion call in the struggle against all manner of half-heartedness. The name given to this periodical was *Cruz y Raya*, a Spanish play on words difficult to translate, meaning at the same time " tabula rasa," " more or less," " yes or no." From being a literary review *Cruz y Raya* developed into a publishing concern. No production, whatever its tendency, was overlooked provided it contained in Bergamin's view some deeper human significance. *Cruz y Raya* published Malraux and Alberti as well as the great Spanish mystics ; the young Spanish and Spanish-American poets as well as a life of St. Catherine of

Siena ; Bergamin's studies on Lope de Vega and editions of the great Spanish classics. There too Bergamin's original work appears, such sparkling productions as *Mangas y Capirates* and *Tres Escenas en Angulo Recto.*

Within a short time *Cruz y Raya* became a sort of clearing-house for all the intellectual cross-currents of Spain and a spiritual source of revolutionary energy in every field. But with politics, in the ordinary sense, Bergamin was not concerned. " When I ask a mathematician or a musician to write about mathematics or music, I am not curious to know whether his political convictions agree with my own. I am too deeply imbued with the fact that all true science, all true art, and all true religion amount in the long run to the same thing : all serve humanity."

In extracts from the great Spanish thinkers and poets (*Las Cosas Claras*), Bergamin has tried to show that this fundamental oneness of all human endeavour runs like a red thread through the whole of Spanish civilization, indeed through civilization itself. " The great tradition of Spain has always been revolutionary. Every system of thought is dialectically built up from two opposites : the conservative will to retain eternally valid truths, and the revolutionary tendency that strives after perpetual progress in the region of the ephemeral.

Our classics were great because they always maintained living contacts with the people, and here in Spain the concept people is synonymous with the concept revolution."

Bergamin sees in this humanism the fundamental principle which, transcending the boundaries of political parties, may become the basis of a united front which is not merely opportunist. " Man is everywhere," he says, " and everything is for man. I am a Christian because in Christ God became a man like myself. If we did not see the man in God it would be impossible for us to be in real communion with Him. Christians and non-Christians can come together on the basis of this common belief in mankind. The purpose of Christianity is the rebirth of man, but it is a remarkable fact that these days I can only talk about the ' new man ' with Communists. Even Nietzsche, for all his hostility to Christianity, was only searching for this ' new man ' in his superman. We too are striving to givc birth to him, and in another shape he constitutes the ever-recurring theme of recent Russian literature. This literature is akin to our ways of thought just because both in Russia and Spain it is thought that given the opportunity the re-birth of man may be effected without delay. But an even closer bond unites us.

" From ancient times mankind has been conversant with the concept of race. Literally race means trail, the trail of the blood that traverses time. They that make an idol of race, after the Nazi fashion, are the slaves of blood's heritage. Christ came, however, in order to redeem us with His blood from this inheritance. He gave His blood to show that blood was not the highest good. Hence, Christianity teaches that faith will become as blood unto us. But the faith and the spirit are one. This is movingly expressed in the holy sacrament of the altar, where we partake of the flesh and blood of the Redeemer, and thereby enter into spiritual contact with Him. Even at the time when it was promised, this sacrament gave umbrage because it was thought to be too material, too concrete ; I had almost said too materialistic. In the Catholic church, however, everything has been ' materialized ' in this fashion ; hence I like to maintain that a Christian cannot be an idealist in the philosophical sense, and that historical materialism stands much closer to us than is generally assumed. After all the spirit must become as flesh and blood unto us. Christ gave His blood in order to release us in spirit from the slavery of race, family, and property. The sacrifice of Christ was a service to mankind, and just because we are Christians, only mankind interests us.

" Malraux is akin to us because in seeking the

limits of human inadequacy, which prevents mankind from becoming truly human, he oversteps them. André Gide is akin to us because his whole work is a voyage to discover future man and his happiness. Karl Marx is akin to us in his pursuit of the material foundations upon which this future humanity can raise itself.

"As a Catholic I am interested in every thinker and reformer who seeks in earnest to give a larger humanity to the life of man. And even though we may differ intellectually on many subjects, I have adopted as my own these words of Malraux: 'We can always agree about life even though we have different opinions on the subject of death.'"

I then asked Bergamin what section of the Spanish public he had been able to reach by means of *Cruz y Raya*. "Only a very small minority of intellectuals," he readily admitted. "Our journal had a circulation of 1,700 copies, of which a very considerable number went to America. The official world, the big dailies, and the Church tried to smother us with their silence, which was worse than coming into the open to fight us. Besides, it should be remembered that taken all in all the intellectual level of the Spanish bourgeoisie was lower than that of any in Europe. On the other hand, my greatest cause for rejoicing has always been the understanding with which my activities have been followed by the simple and illiterate folk of Spain. I still remember the time when I delivered a series of lectures in the Asturias on the subject of Dostoievsky and Cervantes, two Christian writers I am inclined to rate higher than all the rest. The middle class arrived in fair numbers to have a chance of seeing with their own eyes the miracle of a Catholic revolutionary. My address was received with only the faint applause of courtesy. At the back of the hall, however, were some twenty miners, and one of them acting as their spokesman approached the platform in some hesitation to ask a number of questions. It was clear from these questions how deeply they had become engrossed in my lecture, and how their hearts had responded to what their untutored minds had not been able to follow. I remember another occasion when I was invited to Burgos to lecture on the subject of Lope. The Governor made no reply to the request for permission to hold the lecture, thereby avoiding in the most cowardly fashion having to take a decision in the matter. Then it was that the workers of Burgos decided that the meeting should take place in any event, and I addressed them in a theatre that was exclusively filled with proletarians. Upon their own request I avoided every topical subject in order to forestall political complications, and I seldom delivered a more purely philosophical and academic lecture. But when I left the theatre, I crossed the street between two rows of workers, who greeted me with their raised clenched fists. They had entirely identified themselves with my thoughts."

When Bergamin speaks of the people, a glow begins to suffuse his cheeks and an expression almost of ecstasy comes over his face. For him the people are not, as in the Fascist conception, the grey masses of sub-humanity who have to be kept in leash by a small group of rulers; for him the people are the chaos from which a new world is being moulded, the inexhaustible reservoir of forces from which every thinker and poet must draw who does not wish to be cut off from life itself. For him as for Wies Moens in his pre-Fascist days, the general run of the people constitute "the mother of the generations," the origin and cause to which everything that has human significance returns.

When I asked him what place he had reserved for the Church, as an organization, in this system of his, which ever and again postulates the plain simple man of the people, Bergamin's reply was almost naïve. "But what is the Church, if not the people itself, the communion of all who believe in Christian truth? Not in isolation but only as a community can mankind bring about a state of Christian righteousness upon earth. It has been the great error of Protestantism to imagine that man as an individual can find God directly and without being in communion with others. The road to God is perpetual communion with others, and this communion finds its expression in the organization of the Church. The necessity for organizing this community I recognize without reservation, but just because this organization lies in the temporal field, it is subject to error and corruption as is every other worldly organization. Corruption is almost unavoidable as soon as an ecclesiastical organization ventures into a sphere not its own, in other words, as soon as it becomes political. When that moment arrives you get clericalism instead of the clergy, and then, as a vigilant Catholic, it is my task to denounce this monstrous alliance of the Church with the mighty of this earth."

Bergamin's views spring from an entirely different spiritual world from that in which I am accustomed to live. At the same time Bergamin's passion and nobility of soul are the same as have inspired the best Communists of our day. Arraigned before a judge, Bergamin would be as another Dimitrov in the witness-box. My conversation with Bergamin has increased my conviction that supposedly unbridgeable divergencies of opinion are perhaps less fundamental than was once assumed, and that Fascism, for all the evil it has perpetrated in the world, has at any rate produced one good result : it has brought the best spirits from all the progressive parties steadily closer to each other and has united them in a single-minded struggle on behalf of a new and happier human existence.

MADRID, *October 23rd*, 1936.

Yes, the face of Madrid is considerably altered since I wrote my last letter. Returning from Naval Perral our lorries were climbing up along the steep slopes of the Sierra. The icy night wind penetrated through our clothing and our only comfort was provided by the songs of our comrades. The stark white walls of the Escorial wore an eerie look as they rose up out of the darkness. Our lorries were now humming more softly as we descended towards the Madrid tableland, and the temperature was becoming milder. The following day on the boulevards of Madrid we were already basking in the bountiful warmth of Summer. Joy cannot entirely die under this glittering sun. Madrid continues to be a gay city and suggests a feeling of eternal holiday. But the gaiety is restrained ; the gravity of the situation and the measures taken by the Government have induced a spirit of greater dignity. Mola's assertion that he disposes of a fifth secret column inside Madrid is no idle talk. Often provided with faked identity cards and clad in the overalls of the militiamen, the foes of the Republic foregather in the cafés and discuss their plans on the terraces. Sometimes like bravoes they fire under cover of darkness ; during the night our Alianza building was hit seven times by Fascist bullets.

Supervision has been tightened up considerably ; only a few of the café terraces remain open and at ten o'clock in the evening all the theatres and restaurants are closed. After eleven o'clock nobody is allowed in the street without a special permit. All the lights are then extinguished, when they are not painted blue, and pickets are standing at all the corners of the dark streets. During the day there are great demonstrations of women in the town. The watchword is : all the women must get to work to enable all able-bodied men to be employed at the front or at the fortifications of Madrid.

In the evenings our companies march through the streets on propaganda work. Now and then we call a halt and a worker delivers an allocution. We march between rows of clenched fists and the sound of our tramping feet is drowned in the " vivas " of the masses.

The Government are finally taking those measures which are absolutely indispensable. It must be added that they have been long overdue and, now that the situation is very critical, only strong pressure from the masses has brought them about. Since October 10th, unity of command, a matter of the first importance, has at last become a reality. Although training is terribly behindhand and an enormous amount of time is wasted in talk, a very marked improvement is noticeable in army discipline. We no longer walk about with our rifles; we march. We still lack cartridges for regular practice, but on the other hand nobody now leaves for the front who has not fired one or two shots. We have learnt the elementary principles for lining up in skirmishing order, and for seeking cover. Also in this respect, the inadequate knowledge of the instructors is compensated for by the zeal and goodwill of the men. It must be borne in mind that the Spaniards are the most anti-militaristic people in the world, and have had no experience of a world war. For instance, there is as yet not the least realization of the enormous importance of barbed wire as a defence against cavalry attacks.

At long last the normal activities of the entire building trade have been arrested and all the workers put on to constructing lines of defence. This measure has not come a moment too soon. The introduction of ration cards in the last few days has also brought about a big improvement. There is no actual food shortage but the normal supply has been seriously affected by hoarding on the part of those who had the means. It goes without saying that the Government's decree for parcelling out

Fascist land property is of great political importance, although here, too, the Government had long been anticipated in practice by the masses.

My confidence in the revolutionary strength of the masses themselves is enormous, and I marvel at the discipline with which every discussion is postponed until after victory. The old watchword " No pasaran " (They shall not pass) has politically served its purpose ; our new watchword is " Paseremos " (We shall pass).

In broad daylight one is much less conscious of the gravity of the situation ; the streets are as busy as in Amsterdam on a Sunday. Aeroplanes were circling above the city when towards eleven o'clock the crowds streamed into the Español Theatre where a play by Ramon Sender was to be performed, and where Aquillar, Professor in History and Left Parliamentary deputy for Seville, had promised to speak. I must say that Aquillar spoke extraordinarily well ; nor did he hesitate to emphasize the fact that he was addressing us as a Liberal who had never felt any sympathy for Communism. He dwelt upon the incredible patience with which the Spanish people had endured its poverty—a poverty unknown to any other people. Spaniards heaved a sigh of relief when the democratic republic was born, from which at long last improvements could be expected. The measures of the Republic, however, were anything but radical ; even the highest incomes were only taxed fourteen per cent., and the Church with its untold wealth paid no taxes at all. The Jesuit order was dissolved, but the members of the order were allowed to remain quietly in the country. Officers who refused to take the oath to the Republic were placed on the retired list on full pay. But the big landowners and the military clique refused to tolerate even such tentative reforms as were effected. They had recourse to arms, and the lawful Government could only defend itself by turning for support to the proletariat. These critical times had revealed that the true wealth of Spain did not lie hidden in the cellars of the banks, but was to be found in the noble hearts of the Spanish working-class. Aquillar ended his speech with these words : " Our desire was to provide this people of ours with conditions worthy of human beings, such as are normal in every other democracy. We thought to achieve our purpose to the accompaniment of the Riego Hymn." (The National Anthem of the Republic.) " It has since appeared that even the most elementary reforms can only be carried out to the accompaniment of the International."

MADRID, *November 2nd.*

While I was busy reporting upon the physical aspect of Madrid, news was suddenly received from barracks that we were leaving again for the front the following day—which means to-day. As I shall have to be in barracks by nine o'clock, I got up at six just to send you a few more lines. These days in Madrid have passed all too rapidly. After the privations at the front you can imagine what it was to be given a room in the former palace of the Duke of Herida Spinola and, greatest boon of all, a study of my own. How I have worked and how much more couldn't I do under these conditions ! When I leave my room I come upon the other comrades in the hall or rooms downstairs, artists most of them. The revolution has touched them with its gravity and we have all become one great brotherhood.

The day before yesterday quite unexpectedly I had the great good fortune to come upon Ludwig Renn at the Alianza. Hc has landed here without advertisement and without fuss. " I have not come here as a writer but as former staff officer of the old Prussian army," he expressly declared. What a fine fellow he is ! He brims over with cordiality, his simplicity is disarming, and his only wish is to serve under us as a militiaman. What a career ! To have been successively an aristocrat, an antimilitarist, a communist, a prisoner—and now to be here! He is delighted at last to be able to place his military knowledge at the disposal of a people and a cause that are dear to him.

Renn has set himself to work at once and the whole Alianza is helping him. It is an impressive and moving sight to see how these artists and intellectuals, completely forgetful of themselves, are carrying out whatever task is nearest to hand with the greatest possible punctuality, zeal, and ingenuity. Renn's first work was to write short lapidary watchwords in which are laid down the most elementary rules of conduct for the soldier in the field. Artists then got busy illustrating these watchwords, and within less than twenty-four hours the leaflets were got ready. Yesterday evening Renn and a number of Spanish writers held a meeting at party headquarters next to our barracks. There was no distinction between audience and platform. Every word came back charged with the love and passion of hundreds of beating hearts. Maria Theresa Leon looked like a diver preparing to plunge among the surging masses below. Speaking for all the women, the neat and elegant poetess had suddenly become the living, moving embodiment of their anguish, their expectation, and their hopes. These poets in uniform were the brothers of the militiamen in the hall, at whose side they had stood in the trenches, and whose thoughts they were now interpreting. It was not so much a meeting as a public confessional, full of an almost religious ecstasy which was exalting a whole nation. And yet the questions at issue were of the most practical nature : we were debating ways and means of organizing the defence of Madrid to the last man and woman.

The news of our departure is not unexpected. The first, second, and fourth companies went off yesterday, marching in step magnificently and singing as they went. Wives and mothers were standing on the pavement greeting them with the clenched fist. They were also greeting their friends, and neighbours, for most of the men, as is usual, belonged to the district through which they were passing. Small boys were marching along too by the side of their elder brothers and from all the houses, however poor, flags or red rags were flying. So great is the pride and joy that we who are left behind envy our departing comrades. It is a fever in our blood to be back at the front again ; we want to settle our accounts ; we want to break the back of Fascism once and for all. No pasaran !

The hands of my watch are revolving much too quickly. I must be off in ten minutes. I know for certain that nobody will fail : we have our own voluntary, proletarian discipline. Each one of us does his duty in an army where punishment is unknown, where recourse is never had to confinement to barracks and close arrest. We are like a good football team, with the proper team spirit, but without spectators and without personal ambition. We know that we are setting out to meet the heaviest offensive that can be launched by Mola with all his technical resources and steel weapons ; but we know what we are fighting for and that we shall prevail. Tell that to the comrades in Holland.

MADRID, *November* 16*th*.

. . . I have just come out of the trenches, and am as well as I can be in the circumstances. I have lived through such awful days at the front and at the siege of Madrid, that I can't yet write about things with composure.

One thing I will say ; I have thought of you all a great deal these days . . . While we were in danger—a squadron of twelve aeroplanes dropped twenty bombs on our trenches and at Getafe five armoured cars fired at our line for four hours at a stretch—we had not a moment's fear. You see, we were fighting side by side with the finest comrades in the world and, what is even more important, we knew that we were fighting for your future as well.

It is possible that we shall be defeated and, if that should be, the working-classes everywhere, even in Holland, will be faced with a very difficult time. But I know too that the struggle for a new society will not end with our defeat ; it will be resumed by the coming generation. . . .

MADRID, *November 20th.*

Of one thing I am certain : the world has never witnessed anything so frightful as these continual bombardments of an entirely defenceless city of a million inhabitants. Such bestial cruelty as has been perpetrated by an army, which dares to call itself " national," upon the women and children of the country's capital city, has never been seen before. Indeed, it cannot be sufficiently stressed that these bombardments are sheer terrorization. They are not directed against the armed forces, nor do they serve a single military purpose ; they are aimed exclusively at the annihilation of the civilian population. I have seen how bombs were dropped on the slum quarter where the women had brought us their last chunk of bread and the last of their wine ; I shall never be able to forget the wailing and groaning that rose up from the ruins. I have seen the corpses of little children being taken away in lorries, and the torn façades of blocks of houses which revealed the whole misery of workmen's dwellings. Bombs fell morning, noon, and night ; on the Puerta del Sol, the busiest plaza of the town ; on the Don Carlos Hospital ; on the palace of Liria, one of the most famous museums in the city ; even on the cathedral where Franco had declared that mass would be celebrated upon his entry into Madrid. There are days when the whole magical silhouette of the city is obscured in gunpowder smoke, and nights when it is entirely lit up as by Bengal lights.

In spite of all these horrors and although the enemy is scarcely eight kilometres from the Puerta del Sol, although the Fascists have dropped a basket into the city containing the carved-up body of one of our airmen, although death stalks everywhere, life goes on without panic, and with a degree of heroism that can scarcely be imagined.

Nobody thinks of surrender. In all the streets and alleys the young people are building up barricades. If the Fascists march into Madrid they will find a city in ruins that will be defended so long as there is a house left standing.

But they will not march in ! The bestial cruelty of these bombardments is an expression of their impotent rage at our resistance. The proletariat of Madrid realize that they are defending not only themselves but also the peoples of Europe. Are you aware of this in Holland? Are you in spirit with the men, women, and children of Madrid who refuse to be subdued by any terror? When shall we hear Europe's cry of protest against such shameful cruelty, against these "Nationalists," who are so clearly abhorred by their own nation?

MADRID, *November 18th.*

The underlying causes of our retreat from Getafe were deep-rooted, and unavoidable in the case of an army not systematically built up over a period of years but improvised as it were by the proletariat in the space of a few months. There were also the special political circumstances in Spain to be taken into account. Disunity between Anarchists and Communists, who both feared that the opposite party would seize power, led to the appointment of officers not on grounds of military capacity but purely on grounds of political reliability. Furthermore, when military operations began, promotion took place on grounds of proven courage, which in many cases is a very different thing from possessing an insight into military affairs or a capacity for organization. Our captain, for instance, is the most charming fellow in the world. He is twenty years of age, attended school for a year and a half, worked in a factory in his ninth year, took part in his first strike when he was eleven, found himself in prison at fifteen and has since done splendid and illegal work in the youth movement. He is brave, cordial, and full of good-will. But he is only a big child without any authority or military understanding. That our men are brave individually was conclusively proved at Naval Perral and on other occasions. But bravery is not enough. Most of them are like big children who never look ahead ; and, moreover, they are such Anarchists at heart and so anti-militaristic that they view with mistrust any attempt to introduce more military discipline in the army. In this respect, the political commissars are doing good work, and a more rigid conception of unity of command has now also begun to be introduced, but we are still a very long way from constituting a real modern army. To cap it all, our company at Getafe had just been brought up to strength with the help of a large number of fresh volunteers from the villages, who came under fire for the first time.

We received our marching orders at eight o'clock in the evening and until two in the morning there was singing and laughter as if we were setting out on some festive occasion. I must add that on such occasions all drink is forbidden in barracks and that there was, therefore, no question of intoxication. Besides, the men themselves were on their guard : " Mind ! " you heard them say to each other, " if you drink you won't be able to aim straight." At two o'clock that morning our motor buses departed, and in the first drab light of dawn we dropped the first and fourth companies in the trenches. These trenches form part of the fortification works of Madrid and have been constructed in all haste by the women and boys in their spare time and by the workers who are too old to carry arms. From a military point of view they are entirely inadequate, and so narrow that the officers cannot freely move up and down. They are without ledges for resting the cartridges ; there is no means of draining them in rainy weather, and, what is worse, there are no dug-outs where the men can be protected against cold and wind. They too are a typical improvisation.

When the sun rose we found that at about three hundred metres in advance of our line there was a second row of our soldiers in the field. It was a beautiful morning, almost summer weather. Shooting had ceased and we almost had the feeling of spending a day in the country for the sake of our health. I was feverishly studying Spanish from a primer I had bought. A squadron of aeroplanes was bombarding the first line, but we were left in peace. Unfortunately the commissariat was working badly. All that day and the next we got nothing to eat but some dry bread and a small piece of sausage. At midday a motor-car went by with women from the World Committee for Peace. They told us that the bombardment was causing some demoralization in the first line and they distributed among us a few bottles of brandy. I also had a long conversation with two workers of the Scottish ambulance, which is doing splendid work here. The night was icy but we had found some straw in a barn and slept tolerably well under our blankets. The terrain was undulating, so that I was unable to get a view of the line on the right of the road. Since it looked as if we were going to have another very quiet day, our captain had gone to Madrid to obtain blankets and clothes for the men. Suddenly at eleven o'clock heavy rifle-fire broke out in the direction of the first line, and by one o'clock we saw the men quite coolly retreating towards us. We brought them to a halt, and the officers ordered them back into our trench. That was the first big mistake. Our trench was now overcrowded and with demoralized elements to boot. The obvious course would have been to let them constitute a third line behind ours for the protection of the village. At about two o'clock the trouble began in earnest. The enemy opened a heavy bombardment on our line lasting more than two hours without a break. Besides, we were being machine-gunned uninterruptedly from five tanks, or rather armoured cars that were being driven up and down the road, while we had only an armoured train on the railway track and a rubbishy armoured car on the high road, which soon had to be withdrawn. Our two machine-guns dated from the Middle Ages and did not always function. In spite of all this it was remarkable how comparatively little damage was done to our trench by the fire of the enemy. Far worse was the fact that from sheer nervousness our men were continually shooting, although no enemy was yet in sight, except for the armoured cars which were naturally impervious to rifle-fire. Furthermore, most of them shot without aiming correctly and their bullets often hit the ground barely thirty metres from our line. The consequence was that towards evening we began to run short of ammunition and many rifles were out of action. I tried my best to get them to cease firing, but naturally my voice could not reach farther than a good hundred metres. Then came the attack. As the tanks were unable to break through on our sector, they were diverted at about four o'clock towards the right of the high road, where they were successful in breaking through the line at two places. At that moment a panic broke out on the extreme right wing and one of the companies took to its heels. One company dragged along another in its flight, and more especially the men who had no more ammunition or whose rifles no longer functioned abandoned the line in disorder. The officers ordered them to halt but a feeling of comradeship apparently prevented them from shooting at the fugitives, although this might still have brought the retreat to a standstill. The breech was becoming wider every moment and now the retreat began on our left as well. In my sector I held back the men as long as I could, sometimes by persuasion and sometimes by threatening them with my rifle. We held out perhaps a quarter of an hour longer than the others but in the end I found myself alone in the trench with our *alvarez* (second lieutenant), who had come back when I taunted him with cowardice. "We are alone," he said—"Somos solos." At that moment the enemy was about three hundred metres away. I then realized that the game was up and together we fled to Getafe. Near a railway junction we came upon a few officers, and for a few minutes we formed with them a second line of defence; but this position too became untenable. As the sun was setting we saw the Fascist lines slowly approaching. My throat was as dry as leather, and with panting breath we dragged a case of cartridges along with us, which we soon had to drop in order to transport a wounded soldier. His blood was streaming over my hands, and all the time he was wailing, " A car, a car." By the time we had found an ambulance night had fallen. We sought refuge in a house half-way on the road to Madrid, but had scarcely rested half an hour when suddenly we were roused by noise and bustle outside. Standing in the road was a company of our *asaltos*—who are not volunteers but regular troops. I asked them something and apparently they took me for a spy or a Fascist who accidentally had proceeded too far in advance. This was the most terrifying moment of the night : they were already preparing to shoot me. Fortunately I was able to prove by my papers that all was well. I joined them and we marched back in the direction of Getafe, and with about a hundred men took up our positions on the road. There we lay throughout the following morning without reinforcements, and with nothing to eat but some raw tomatoes we found growing in the field. I felt that this would be the end if it came to an attack. Nevertheless my exhaustion was so great that I fell asleep in a furrow on the roadside. Suddenly I was awakened by somebody vigorously shaking me, and then I saw the kind, genial face of our Sergeant Rubio who was leaning over me. I don't think I ever was so happy in my life. With him I rejoined our company in Madrid.

That same evening we marched with our reconstituted company to Villa Verde Bajo, where a battery had been set up which we had received instructions to defend. While a portion of our company occupied the trenches, the remainder was accommodated in the kiln of a brickyard. You could not imagine a more fantastic sight. Owing to the heat we fell asleep at once, but barely two hours later the artillery changed position, and we were removed to the cellars of a sort of castle, the towers of which we used as an observation post for our artillery. It was scarcely daylight when this was spotted by the enemy who immediately rained shells upon us. We received orders to withdraw behind the embankment of a railway. Since half our company were by this time without cartridges, Pepe was at a loss to know what to do. I advised him to send back to Madrid those of his men who were running short of cartridges and to go forward with the rest. This he endeavoured to do but lacked the necessary authority. Just then a further calamity overtook us : somewhere at the front a second break-through had occurred, and masses of troops in flight were streaming away in our direction. I felt instinctively that no real danger was threatening and

I tried to persuade Pepe to go forward with our company, to stop a senseless panic. Whereupon a corporal suggested that we should go forward ourselves in the hope that the others would follow.

No more than six, however, came along with us. With our small patrol we advanced about four kilometres through the fields and across the deserted trenches, until finally we found on the Cadiz road a detachment of about forty men who were defending this line of communication. They were wild with delight that we had come and, joining up with them, we contrived with our rifle-fire to keep the enemy outside Villa Verde Alto during the whole afternoon. Towards evening reinforcements arrived, and the commandant gave us permission to withdraw in order to go in search of our own company. That evening was perhaps even more terrible than the evening before. Wherever we went, we found straying groups of militiamen without weapons or without ammunition, hungry, officerless, and not knowing wherc to go. The railway which we were skirting had been bombed and the station was a mass of smoking ruins. Dozens of aeroplanes were circling in the crimson sky. Again and again the airmen swooped down low over the field decimating the fleeing militiamen with their machine-guns. Bombs were dropping like hail, and pillars of smoke and flame were rising up from every village within sight. Within a few minutes all that was left of the model garden suburb of the railway workers was a smouldering ruin. Fermin, who was with me the whole day, was saying, " They have taken Madrid," and I too felt at that moment that there was no alternative but to blow out my brains. But the urge to live prevailed over despair ; besides, I had gradually collected as we went along a number of men of our company who had lost their heads. I formed with them a small platoon and marched them back as quickly as possible to our barracks at the Puente de Vallecas to obtain fresh instructions. The commandant took the view that what I had to report was of such importance that he took me in a car straight to headquarters. I was greatly relieved to find that there they had lost their heads much less than I had thought. Although the break-through of the Fascists was a very serious matter, it had taken place on so small a front that they were in danger of soon finding themselves in a pocket. After reporting all I knew, I was given a good bath and the first warm food I had had for four days ; I returned to barracks a different person. Next day Domela and the others also arrived in barracks. During the night they had defended the same road to Cadiz where we had been at midday.

It may sound strange, but the following days of comparative rest were the worst so far experienced.

Our company was occupying a trench behind the Manzanares ; meanwhile the enemy had altered the direction of his attack, and was proceeding more towards the South in the neighbourhood of the Casa del Campo. We were being continually harassed, but only by artillery and by aeroplanes. There was a moment when it looked as if they could not fail to get us for two shells landed in the breastwork of our trench, one of them two metres and the other one metre from the spot where Domela, Pepe, and I were crouching. We were completely covered in earth ; fortunately they failed to burst or I would not be writing to you now. Barely five minutes later a squadron of aeroplanes arrived, and when I saw dozens of bombs dropping like white eggs in our direction, I decided that all was over. They were, however, deflected by the wind and burst twenty metres away. But when I say that we were now going through the worst, I am not referring to all this, which is in the normal routine of warfare and all in the game.

About two hundred metres behind our line lies one of the most frightful slum districts of Madrid ; it is without drains or water-main, and you may remember my description of its inhuman misery in *Een huis zonder vensters.* The loving-kindness with which we were received in this slum is not to be described. A little old woman came up to us with her last chunk of bread and the remainder of her wine, and as she was about to . . .

Telephone call, report immediately to barracks, leaving for the front . . .

UNIVERSITY CITY

November 24th, 1936.

SO HERE WE ARE AT THE FRONT AGAIN, AND A more astonishing front you cannot conceive : we are barely eight minutes from the underground station of Quatro Caminos ! The problem of transporting our company to the front was child's play ; we simply took the underground. At the same time you will see how fearfully dangerous the Fascist break-through has been ; it has brought them literally to the gates of Madrid, although in this direction their front only constitutes an extraordinarily narrow wedge.

I had to interrupt my previous letter just as I was about to tell you that what strikes me as the worst of all is the frightful and entirely needless suffering of the non-combatants. Indeed, it is obvious that the enemy concentrates the greater portion of his bombs and shells almost exclusively, and with the greatest refinement of cruelty, not upon points of strategic importance, but upon working-class districts where he hopes to spread fear and panic.

I was telling you about this district behind our lines, where only the poorest of the poor live. They came out to provide us with all that was left to them in the way of supplies and belongings. They wanted to give us everything, their poor miserable chickens, their blankets, their mattresses, their tomatoes. They sewed on our buttons for us, washed our clothes, looked after us as if we had been their own children. It goes without saying that we refused to endanger their lives by quartering troops in their district; our trenches were at least 300 metres away. Nevertheless, the enemy bombed their poverty stricken hovels with sadistic delight. From our trench we could hear the fearful shrieks of their victims. When all was over, we carried away from the crumbling ruins the little bodies of children who had sat upon our knees, and the mangled bodies of women who had looked after us.

In the trenches you have a rifle in your hand and at any rate the illusion that you can defend yourself; in a city all you can do is to wait and see whether the next bomb will not drop upon your own house and your own family. I believe I cannot recall anything more moving than the sight of the packed underground stations where the population of the suburbs seek refuge, and where women and children live for days and nights, sleeping on some sacking or blankets. There is no end to this terrorization. As soon as the sun shines, twenty, thirty, even forty enemy aeroplanes circle above the city dropping their bombs and, when it is overcast, the enemy batteries hurl their incendiary bombs in haphazard fashion all over the capital. In these circumstances I cannot think of a greater mockery than to speak of the conscience of the world. Even the hordes of Attila never destroyed their own capital or used their weapons to exterminate the women and children of their own people.

FRENTE DE L'ESTACION DE GOYA

December 10th, 1936.

ABOUT FOUR WEEKS AGO WHEN THE ENEMY BROKE through our lines, first at Getafe and then at Villa Verde, I thought for a moment that all was lost, and I was not alone in thinking so. I had seen our scattered companies decimated by the machine-gun fire of the low flying Heinkels. As we went by, villages and stations were bursting into flames and collapsing under shell-fire. Everything that stood in the way of the Moorish cavalry was cut down and our troops were thrown back to the bridge of the Princesses and the bridge of the French. I maintain that in those days it was the women who saved Madrid. They literally chased back to the front the men who were seeking refuge in their homes; they themselves picked up the rifles that had been thrown away and defended the entrance to the town from behind hastily thrown-up barricades. It soon became clear that the stampede of the previous days could not be ascribed to cowardice on the part of the militiamen; it bore all the characteristic marks of an unreasoning panic. They who had fled the previous days now streamed back to their companies, not only offering resistance, but actually launching a counter-offensive under infinitely more difficult circumstances. With boundless bravery and at the cost of frightful sacrifices, they succeeded in definitely checking the enemy's further progress and in winning back a number of important positions. I cannot sufficiently insist upon the fact that our militiamen are the finest and bravest material it is possible to imagine, provided they are well led. In many respects, however, they are mere children, and extraordinarily susceptible to psychological influences when energetic leadership is lacking or the officers lose their heads. When later they recover their balance, their very sense of shame induces them to perform the maddest acts of bravery in order to make good. The days of Getafe and Villa Verde were also the days when boys like Col, armed only with a few hand-grenades, captured one enemy tank after the other.

It was on a Saturday that Franco announced on the wireless that next day he would drink his coffee in Madrid. Radio Lisbon was already describing how he had entered the town in triumph on a white charger. At Avila the Council of Blood that was to take over the administration of the city had already been appointed. Foreign journalists were forbidden to accompany the army because Franco wished to be alone when settling accounts with the population of Madrid. Mola was already foreseeing a repetition of Badajoz and proclaimed the death penalty for anybody found with weapons in his hand. . . . Four weeks have now gone by and, meanwhile, Franco's coffee has turned cold. All of them were wrong because they did not know the proletariat. They did not know that the proletariat are capable of making mistakes but that they profit by these mistakes. They can be beaten, but they will arise refreshed after each defeat ; they may blench for a moment, but they will resume the struggle with correspondingly greater courage and conviction. No wonder our enemies in their headlong course broke their bleeding heads against the recovered heroism of the proletarians of Madrid.

The defence of our positions hinges partly upon an armoured train, which in the event of a heavy attack can be rushed from Madrid within a few minutes. With a view to being able to summon this train in time, a field telephone was hastily laid on. When the telephone was installed and the engineers had withdrawn, it was discovered that there was a lack of contact somewhere and that it did not function. There we lay for more than three days before somebody finally came to restore the contact. All this time we had fine fun with the telephone that did not work. The captain, the *alvarez*, the sergeants, and whoever had to go to company headquarters, played at telephoning. They rang up their best girl or their mother-in-law ; they ordered a dinner with champagne in the city ; they held imaginary conversations with Mola or Queipo de Llano himself in mostly unprintable language. This telephone seemed to me a symbol, not only of the militiamen's most valuable quality, but also of their greatest weakness : a cheerful nonchalance, which induces an invariable liveliness and buoyancy of spirit, but which also inclines them all too often to neglect what is absolutely essential until it is too late.

A cheerful nonchalance. . . . As we were marching from the University City to our new positions, a boy of fifteen acted as our guide. For the space of an hour we marched in darkness through suburbs where every house had been damaged more or less by thc bombardment and abandoned. The poles of the electric trams had snapped. The wires were hanging low over the street ; shells had dug deep craters in the pavement, and everywhere fragments of broken glass were glittering in the moonlight. Our young guide was from the south, and Pepe said to him, " Antonio, sing something to us. The lieutenant would like to hear one of your flamencos."

As we were marching on to where the machine-guns were barking like mad dogs, the boy began to sing. All conversation in the company was stilled. His tender high-pitched boyish voice had the crystal purity of the moon. The melody put one in mind of Arab songs, and then again of an old Gregorian chant. The text, which he was improvising as he went along was very simple : " Our brave militiamen, they will surely win ; oh ! how happy we shall be when our militiamen win ! " I was reminded of a little bird at Getafe that had calmly settled upon a tree, while the battle was at its fiercest, unruffled by the bullets. We turned a corner in pitch darkness, and immediately the rattling of the machine-guns seemed closer, harsher, and more cruel. " Bend down," commanded the captain ; " extend to five paces, double march to the trench." We were in the firing-line and the boy's song suddenly broke off like a bit of glass.

The enemy is about 800 metres away from us, in a trench running from the Military Hospital to the Estremadura road. He occupies the small village opposite, and we can clearly see the holes in the houses behind which he has installed his machine-gunners. His artillery, which must be somewhat farther back, engages our positions for a few hours every afternoon. The marksmanship is bad and most of the shells burst in the cemetery a hundred metres behind our line. It looks as if the dead were to be denied their peace ; perhaps the Fascist slogan " Spain, awake ! " is for their benefit as well.

Great damage has been done to the workmen's houses that constitute our line together with the trench. Holes through which we can fire in the event of an attack have been bored in every wall ; the moon peers through the broken tiles of the roofs ; the smashed window-panes have been replaced by boards that shut out the light. In the evenings, by the reeking flame of an oil wick, dark shadows play upon the broken furniture and our quarters wear a spectral air. A bridal couple on the wall stares at us from out of a gilt frame half hidden in cobwebs, and a broken gramophone still testifies to a modest pretence at well-being. Two militiamen are busy chopping up an old chair for firewood. Some tattered books have been swept in a corner. Everything about us is filthy, dusty, broken, neglected. The husky yelping of hungry dogs left behind in the houses farther up echoes through the night.

We have been living in these ruins for the last twelve days. Everything we touch is dirty ; even the water from the well is muddy and leaves a grey deposit in our glasses. It is too cold to have a good wash. The pavement in front of our house, the only bit of the street that is not in the line of fire, is impassable owing to the excrement of 140 soldiers. We haven't been out of our clothes these twelve days. Three times we have had to beat off a night attack, and we are on duty eight hours a day. Most of us have no decent boots left and throughout these two weeks we have not once had a warm meal, since the cook-wagon is unable to cross the line of fire. Nevertheless, I have not heard a single complaint. In the evenings, as we sit round the fire with running eyes, we tell each other stories from *Tyl Eulenspiegel* or *Ali Baba and the Forty Thieves*, and we often break into song. Nobody has any doubts of victory. Yesterday a bullet crushed the shoulder-blade of our little Manuel. Thomas has been hit in the thigh by a shrapnel splinter. " Qué suerte ! " the comrades say, " our luck is in ; here we've been a whole week and we're all alive ! "

Often they come and say to me, " Now tell us, *teniente*, what really made you come here ? " I shrug my shoulders. " You fellows should know the reason by this time. I came because the fight you are putting up also concerns us."—" Yes," they say, " we know all about that, but that fellow over there comes from the village ; you must explain it properly to him." I then produce a map, and show them that, if the Fascists win in Spain, France will be encircled on all sides. " With Spain as a jumping-off ground, Germany can cut England off from her colonies. That is the moment when the world war should break out under the most favourable conditions possible for Fascism. That is why we are defending here not only Spain, but democracy, and even the frontiers of the Soviet Union." They then look at me with flashing eyes and say, " Qué lucha ! "—" What a struggle ! "

During these last weeks, I have repeatedly witnessed aerial combats in which enemy machines were shot down by our small chasers and, according to the papers, they must be suffering considerable losses. Nevertheless—and I hope I may be wrong—it often appears to me that the numerical preponderance of the enemy in the air goes on increasing. The squadron that flew yesterday over our positions on its way to Madrid was the biggest I have ever seen. I counted thirty-nine monster bombers protected by twenty chasers. They now no longer trouble to bomb our trenches, knowing well the extreme difficulty of hitting our long thin line ; besides, even the biggest bomb only does moderate damage owing to the zigzags of the trench. And so, without worrying about us, they set their course directly for Madrid, which provides them with a far surer target. Madrid may not be particularly attractive once you are there, but seen from our positions its pure white silhouette suggests some fairy city on the hills. Then the aeroplanes approach, the earth rumbles with the dull thud of explosions, and five minutes later the whole city has disappeared behind a cloud of dust and smoke. Even the telephone skyscraper is obscured to the view. Our men lie impotently in the trench. Nobody speaks but all are wondering whether the bombs have not fallen on their own district: whether their wife, their mother, their brother are still alive at this moment. They will only know after the company has spent its two full weeks at the front and returns on leave to the devastation of Madrid. Nevertheless, I have not met with anybody in our company who was made to falter by this terrorism. On the contrary, every bombardment fans the flames of hatred and increases the determination to win. "The reason being," says Fermin to me, "that from the very beginning we have known that our only choice lay between death and victory. Each one of us is a volunteer, and we all know what we are fighting for. We are a backward people, so far as knowledge goes, but we are not to be deceived in our hearts."

That Fermin was right appeared only a few days later when the enemy again scattered thousands of leaflets over our lines. Naturally, it occurred to nobody to prevent these leaflets from being picked up and read. On the contrary, officers and men ran like hares to gain possession of them. Then we had a good laugh. It really was a jolly afternoon. I remember Juan Antonio, of the fourth platoon, an illiterate who insisted upon having the leaflet read to him three times over by three different people. He gave me a questioning look. "Qué tonterias!" he said, "What tomfoolery is this? Is it possible that they can be so stupid?" And indeed the curious blend of effrontery, cynicism, and fantastic lying which characterizes not only such leaflets but also the wireless addresses of Franco or of the drunken Queipo de Llano—we hear them often over Radio Burgos or Seville—is so palpably at variance with the facts that even the simplest illiterate has sufficient experience of life not to be deceived for one moment.

How is it, then, that their propaganda is so clumsy? The reason must be that those responsible for it have always been out of touch with the people, and are themselves taken in by delusions which fear and prejudice have conjured up. They genuinely believe that "the people" are a "stupid, red rabble," and their morbid imagination ascribes cruelties to us which only spring from the sadism of their own wishful dreaming. Never having suffered themselves, they cannot understand the infinite tenderness, the deep compassion born of suffering, that make up the soul of the people. Since the pursuit of pelf and power is the mainspring of their lives, they cannot grasp that we may be driven to struggle for motives other than sheer greed. Where ministries of propaganda are set up for the systematic dissemination of falsehood, it is useless to expect an understanding for the primitive feeling for truth which continues to inhabit the simple heart of a peasant. Franco's propaganda leaflets might have made an impression upon a Dutch middle class public ; his mistake was to distribute them among the proletarians of Spain.

With voices trembling with indignation, they would come up to me and read a sentence or two : " Spaniards, while you are enduring hunger, your Government are paying the highest salaries to foreign adventurers, who with weapons in their hands are bent upon turning your country into a Russian colony." Others indulged in mockery. " I say, José, when we are back in Madrid, you'll stand us drink, won't you ? We did not know you were a millionaire."

All this is part of the fairy tale of the Russian roubles which the bourgeoisie so readily swallow because they themselves think it a sign of madness not to be actuated by money motives.

Our boys know that Franco began the fight with the assistance of Moorish mercenaries, with the soldiers of the Foreign Legion, and with Italian and German Fascists who were disguised in the uniform of the latter. They know, because they are in the movement themselves, that we are not paid for our articles, our work, our propaganda for the party. They know that the foreign volunteers have often had to overcome the greatest difficulties in getting to Spain, that they have been promised nothing, and that they need expect no pecuniary advantages. Hence the cordiality, love, and admiration that goes out to us foreigners, and often fills us with embarrassment.

The Spaniards are a people of minstrels and story-tellers ; they are already weaving legends around the International Battalion, as they sit round their reeky log-fires of an evening. In these stories, the soldiers of the International Battalion are already being transfigured into demi-gods and are compared to the Cid and the knightly heroes who once expelled the Moors from Spain. In fact, the narrator often seems to forget that he too has already spent five months at the front, although it must be granted that the boys of the International Battalion, stationed always at the most threatened sectors, have set an example to all of courage, self-sacrifice, and discipline.

Domela and I receive our full share of the love and friendship showered upon all foreigners. When we were last on leave I was invited to have some food with a few comrades in Vallecas. I hesitated, knowing how scanty the food had become for the civilian population. My comrades, however, had quietly drawn up a little plan of their own. They took me along with them from one house to the other, and, whatever I might say, I had to take my place at table in each house. " You see," they said laughing, " if you had had food only with one of us, you would still have been hungry when you got up, but with the four of us you will have had just enough."

A few days later Domela said to me, " Haven't you noticed that our evenings' rations have recently been larger ? "—" Yes," I said, " the commissariat is apparently improving." Domela shook his head. " I think it's getting rather worse, but we get more than the others." And, true enough, we again received that evening a double portion of ham. We complained to the captain, whose face assumed an air of mystery. " Don't you meddle with what doesn't concern you ; that's quite in order." We protested with energy that we did not think it in order at all. It turned out that the militiamen, while we had gone to the Academy one evening, had got together and decided that the two foreigners had to receive double rations, " because the portions we are getting at the moment are absolutely insufficient, now that the warm food is not coming through." It goes without saying that, with all appreciation for their good intentions, we refused to go on receiving double rations at the expense of the others.

Whenever we return to Madrid from the front, we find that the havoc has increased. It makes one's eyes fill with tears to see the terrible scars that deface a city once so gay ; the smoking ruins of the National Library, of the Don Carlos Hospital, and of the simple workmen's dwellings. Beside me, however, the comrades were singing : " Los esclavos el triunfo alcanzaran ! " (" The slaves shall achieve their triumph ! ") For them, the worst is not fear for their own lives, but the uncertainty as to the lot of their children, their wives, and their parents while they are in the trenches. . . . Efforts are being made to evacuate the non-combatants from Madrid. 300,000 have already been removed to the provinces. But the population of the city, which already exceeded a million, has been enormously increased by all the refugees from the villages. Only two roads lead to Valencia, and the available transport is absolutely inadequate. I have seen women and children being packed in open lorries, and an old taxi holding ten. If there were a particle of humanity left in Europe, immediate steps would be taken to send lorries—though that would be no sovereign remedy. Even in the villages of the interior and the smiling towns along the coast the refugees are not safe. I have seen the battered façades of the hotels of Alicante, which had been transformed into crèches : a German cruiser was lying in harbour with all its lights on in order to facilitate their bombardment by the rebel ships. Bergamin was telling me that his six-year-old boy was lying in his little bed by the window when they opened fire. " He had the presence of mind to get up at once and rush to the cellar. Had he remained five minutes longer, he would have been buried under the collapsing ceiling. My wife endured mortal anxiety because she was unable to open the door of his room." Meanwhile, the poster showing the mutilated bodies of Spanish children is considered " offensive " and may not be pasted up on the town hoardings in Holland. Our authorities do not appear to be particularly outraged by the crime itself ; perhaps they think the children of the Reds suffer less. . . .

PUENTE DE SAN FERNANDO, *January 28th.*

While I have been away, great changes have taken place in our battalion. The reorganization of the army is being seriously taken in hand, and, instead of the old arbitrary units, we have now as in every other army, brigades of a specified size. For instance, our original battalion has now been split up into two brigades, and to my great regret, I have not been transferred to my old company, but to the fourth of the Manolo Battalion. I venture to think, however, that my comrades regretted it even more than I. This morning they had to move forward and they all began nudging me, saying that I had to come too. Many of them had tears in their eyes. There and then they held a meeting and addressed a joint communication to headquarters demanding my return.

To please them I marched out with them to the front. You should have seen how they set out! Singing throughout the journey, well dressed, with red flags attached to their rifles, you would have thought they were going to a feast. So it is always and, though soaked through and through and covered in mud, the company that has been relieved returns from the front in an equally festive mood. When they reach the bridge of Vallecas, you should see the joy with which the children make a dash for their father, how the women keep step with them. We are greeted by all the tram-conductors, and people wave at us from the windows of every house.

After six months of war, cold, hunger and bombardment, there is no falling off in morale, no trace of defeatism, no weariness. In the courtyard of our barracks, the new volunteers who have recently arrived from their villages are being exercised. A number of new gay posters cover the walls of the houses. It looks as if the streets were packed more than ever with people and transport. The flag of the Republic is waving on the battered buildings. Soldiers are singing the latest satirical songs improvised by themselves, and under the large portraits of La Pasionaria the slogan is scrawled in letters of flame

No Pasaran !
Pasaremus !

Between the positions occupied by the Perreira and the Durutti Battalions, there are no trenches and the terrain is very broken. Here at night we set up listening posts along the little stream and behind the trees. The others know about this and it is along the bed of this stream that deserters from the enemy camp regularly come over to us, sometimes three, sometimes as many as five in one night. Upon one occasion twenty crossed over. The day before yesterday they brought along with them a splendid new type of anti-aircraft machine-gun and another earlier in the week. They creep up on their knees until they are quite close to our line and then they clap their hands so that we may be sure they cannot throw hand-grenades. They all are a fearsome sight, with their long beards and their clothes hanging like rags from their body. Their bones seem to rattle with hunger. They fall upon the bread we give them and clasp the tins of preserves as if they would never let go of them. Then, when they are brought along to us, it is grand to see the militiamen dash up from all sides to embrace them. There is laughter and tears; they are pelted with cigarettes, and meanwhile a few of the boys are already going round with their forage-cap: "For they must have some pocket money when they go to Madrid." When they have somewhat recovered, the deserters begin to talk. They say that they were dragged from their villages and compelled to take service; that almost half their men consist of Portuguese, who have been sent by the Salazar Government; that for three months they have not seen one centimo of pay, and that a soldier who asked for a blanket was punished by being stripped and made to do duty in that condition for a whole night.

Behind us we hear the whirring of a car. The propaganda service has been warned by telephone, and the loud speaker has arrived. We shove the big wooden monster as far out as possible towards the enemy lines and place the wires well behind at a safe spot where the microphone is set up. The Spanish national anthem, the air of Riego, blares through the night.

" Atencion ! Atencion ! "

One of the comrades begins his allocution. The enemy replies with angry rifle-fire in the direction of our wooden monster. Its voice, however, is louder than that of the machine-gunners. " Workers on the other side, why do you fight against your comrades ? " When he has finished, another repeats his address in Portuguese, and then an Arab addresses the Moors.

By this time, firing has almost entirely ceased.

" Now you will hear some of your own men, who this very night have crossed over to our side." Complete silence reigns as one of the deserters begins to speak.

" They have not shot us down, they have given us food and clothing. They have treated us like human beings—do you hear ?—like human beings, human beings. And that sergeant of ours who threatens with his revolver, you must shoot him down, and you must do what we have done, for those you call the Reds are human beings. But those officers of ours, Franco and the whole lot of them, they are *hijos de puta* (sons of bitches), and they jolly well won't take Madrid ! "

Our soldiers are jubilant ; they laugh, they cry, and run alongside the car that is taking our two new comrades to the city.

FRENTE EL PARDO, *March 21st*, 1937.

Ya vuelve la Primavera,
Suena la gaita,—ruede la danza :
Tiende sobre la pradera
El verde manto de la esperanza

(The Spring is returned,
Let the hornpipe sound—on with the dance ;
The green mantle of hope
Is spread over the fields.)

Is it quite by accident that my eye should have hit upon this spring song of an old Spanish poet this morning, upon opening my primer again after so long? I could not resist reading it out to the sergeant, who had brought me his morning report, and we both had to laugh. " Sopla caliente la brisa "—Softly the breezes blow—so sings the poet ; but here, at Las Rosas, it would seem as if the ice-cold North wind had only dropped so that the ice-cold rain could fall more fiercely. But perhaps elsewhere there are already intimations of the coming of spring. About ten days ago I was given a few hours' leave to get myself measured in Madrid for a new uniform, which is now compulsory for officers. By the bridge of San Fernando, a machine-gun trained its fire upon our car. We dashed up the winding slope at a tearing pace. Through the little window I just had time to see several trees in bloom. I think it was almond blossom. But Madrid itself was desolate with rain and from our trenches up to the wooded fringe of the Pardo there was nothing to be seen but muddy fields ploughed up and neglected. Ah, these poets !

> La flor rie en su capullo ;
> Suene la gaita—ruede la danza :
> Canta el agua en su murmullo
> El poder santo de la esperanza.
>
> (The flower is smiling in the bud ;
> Let the hornpipe sound, on with the dance ;
> The bubbling water sings
> Of hope's holy strength.)

But the water that drips through the roof of my shelter on to this paper and is drenching my mattress sings a very different sort of ditty. Inspired by Piforver I have been trying to render the opening lines :

The early blossom hangs from every tree,
And budding green sprouts forth between dead moss ;
In no-man's land a corpse lies dreaming,
The flesh already dropping from dry bone.

A smell of thyme is in the languorous wind,
A paler blue pervades the tepid air,
I strive to find the lice within my shirt
And give it up as the wind rises.

A bird is singing somewhere in the wood,
Outpouring from the heart its youth and gladness ;
Fiercely a bullet whistles past my ear
And, in the nick of time, I duck my head.

No, I can't do it ; nothing will come of it. I feel like a marmot in this cold and would like to hibernate. I have lost all zest in things. I can't read. I don't even feel like playing chess with Domela : the mental effort is too great. Like an animal, all I can do is to lie in wait for my food that should arrive at seven o'clock, and hope it will not have turned too cold on the way.

We used to cry shame on the turf huts of the Drente heath. They are palaces, however, compared with what we have here. Even the lot of the cave-men was better than this. One feels they would have scorned to live in a shelter, where water rises from the ground, with a gas-mask on that makes one's head feel like bursting after an hour. Besides, they had their wives and children with them, they ate roast haunch of venison and drank beer, even though it might be out of the skulls of the defeated foe. What we eat and drink is primarily mud.

Far away in the distance, like a *fata Morgana*, Madrid lies upon its hills ; but it is just as inaccessible as if it were at the other end of the world. Our trench is like a small island in a sea of mud. When it is dark we try to extend it towards the Pignatelli position. It is a hopeless task, and little progress is made. We sink deep in the clay ; on all sides water bubbles up from the subsoil, and, lacking the necessary tools, we tear up the sticky blocks of clay with our hands.

Our only connecting link with the world is the newspaper ; it sometimes reaches us two or three days late, but we get it, and for the last few days the news is consistently favourable. It is a miracle that we have been able to repel the fifth great offensive against Madrid. Mussolini's troops, for all their magnificent up-to-date equipment, have been beaten by a handful of simple Spanish workers. Madrid is not Addis Ababa. The Roman vulture will have to seek its victims elsewhere, and hope is returning to our weary breasts. Once more I open my little book and find that the poet was not entirely wrong after all, although the Spring is yet to come.

Morirá la primavera ;
Suene la gaita—ruede la danza :
Mas cada año en la pradera
Tornará el manto de la esperanza.

(Spring will die
Let the hornpipe sound—make room for
the dance :
Hope with mantle green
Shall every year cover the fields anew.)

Basta ; enough for to-day. It is easier for me to think of you all than to write to you, or play at writing verse.

March 23rd.

Needless to say we are enormously pleased with our great victory at Guadalajara. It is a resounding slap in the face for international Fascism, and it was high time too ! All the same, things are not quite what they were as regards human material. The levies that are now being raised are no longer of the same quality as the volunteers of the first days. As in every war, the greatest losses have been endured by the best forces. It is also becoming increasingly more difficult for Madrid, with its million inhabitants, to supply its army with the necessary foodstuffs. Our rifles are wearing out because we have no means of keeping them clean, and new rifles are not to be got, owing to non-intervention. We are now without sugar, and salt is scarce. We are often short of tobacco, and in

Madrid women and children are living on the border-line of famine. Tell the Dutch workers that we require foodstuffs and fuel, but in the first place lorries and petrol.

MADRID, *March* 28th.

You may want to hear about my personal experiences, but there is nothing very special or very heroic to report.

We were at the front for more than a month and an attack was expected. Nothing happened, however, and apart from our daily death-roll from enemy rifle-fire we enjoyed the peace that is usually expressed in the communiqué by the words : " From the front there is no news of importance."

An icy wind was blowing from the Sierra, the rain was dripping through the roof of our primitive shelter, the trench was filled with mud, and the straw on which we were sleeping gradually became soaked with ground moisture. The confidence and good spirits of our militiamen remained imperturbable. We knew that the enemy were attacking on the Jarama and at Guadalajara with an enormous preponderance of armament, and we knew that our lines of communication with Valencia were threatened. But nobody was anxious ; nobody doubted for an instant that we should be successful in beating them off. Our optimism proved justified ; we read with inexpressible delight a few days later that our troops at Guadalajara had defeated not only Franco's Fascists, but Mussolini himself. We were wild with enthusiasm but life in the trenches went on as if nothing had happened : the cold, the boredom, the dirt, and our almost daily casualties continued to be with us.

And then, upon a blessed evening, we suddenly had the news that we were being relieved and had been given four days leave in Madrid.

How can I get you to understand what that wonderful word, Madrid, means to us ? For you, Madrid is the city with two thousand dwellings in ruins, the city over which the grey shadow of death perpetually hangs, the city transformed by privation and misery into the world's noblest monument of martyrdom.

And for us ?

For those who were born in Madrid, it means family, friends, the joy of reunion, and a mother's embrace. For those who come from the villages, it means a glass of wine in a good café, light, music, a cinema or a theatre, a night's sleep in a bed with blankets, a bath, a night when at long last one can take off one's boots.

It also means something more ; it means the town

for which we have suffered and fought, the symbol of world opposition to Fascism, the city we have grown to care for as one cares for a child that has given much trouble. And I understand the French volunteer who said to me yesterday five minutes after a shell had burst in the central quarter and while the corpses were still lying in the street : " Here in Madrid I feel at home as if I were in Paris again."

We have left the mud and the woods behind us ; we see the first trams, the first open shops, men standing at the counter of a small café. How will the city receive us ? An old feeling comes back to me again. I remember what we felt when after our night-shift the cage brought us up from the Emma coalmine in Dutch Limburg, how we asked ourselves as the first grey light fell into the shaft whether it was raining or whether the sun would shine. I am also reminded of the days when I would be standing on the forecastle after months of sailing, looking out towards a port that came in sight.

I must say that upon this occasion the city gave us a royal reception. The sun was shining in every street ; it was shining even upon the shell-shattered houses where children were playing among the ruins. But we were not only basking in the warmth of the first sun of springtime ; it was the joyous sun of happiness and hope that was filling many a heart after our magnificent victory at Guadalajara.

How can a militiaman on leave best spend the few precious hours that are vouchsafed to him? I pick up a newspaper. Innumerable films of excellent quality invite me; but would it not be better to take the opportunity to hear some good music again? There is a splendid concert to-night, and at the Español they are giving Electra. Unable to make up my mind I roam the streets. The shops have an alluring air; masses of people are streaming into the department stores, where they are having a clearance sale. I have again the feeling of being a paid-off seaman, whose dearest wish is to squander all his money that very afternoon. But what about books? It is ages since I read anything worth while, and here they are for sale for a few pesetas in hundreds of little barrows along the streets. Or shall I attend the big meeting that is being organized to-day by the Social Democratic Party and join in the enthusiastic crowds?

Pasted on the wall of one of the schools of the Alerta youth movement, beside a wall newspaper, I saw a poster scrawled in a childish hand announcing a big fete of youth in the Fuencaral Cinema. I paid my peseta to go in and found myself at once in the atmosphere of the happiest of children's parties. The hall was full of young people of all ages, many of them with their parents. During the pauses there was a buzz of many voices and much singing. From the balconies many paper aeroplanes went fluttering down at the same time as manifestoes announcing the big congress at which the amalgamation of the entire youth of Madrid was to become an accomplished fact. The stage was occupied by boys and girls of seventeen and eighteen years of age in gaily coloured Spanish costumes. They were performing a play full of childlike spirit and humour, in which no revolutionary tendency was noticeable. That same afternoon I went to the cinema, attracted by the name of the film " Abyssinia " which put me in mind of our watchword of a few days ago: " Madrid is not Addis Ababa." When the Negus appeared on the screen he was greeted with applause and somebody from the gallery cried out, " We shall continue your struggle and win." Then followed the Spanish anti-war film, " Men against Men ", showing incredible war scenes which would certainly not be passed by the censor of any other country. It was a fierce onslaught against all the fomenters of war, and the public, composed mainly of militiamen on leave like myself, applauded. They knew all about these horrors; they had experienced them in their own bones and to-morrow they would be going back to that hell. But this indictment of war they applauded from the bottom of their hearts. These men who trounced the Italians remain pacifists ; they are waging war only to prevent the world war upon which Fascism is bent ; they are giving their lives to save the lives of the whole generation that comes after them.

That evening I had my meal at the Gran Via Hotel, where foreigners, journalists, savants, film stars, and airmen foregather, as well as officers and men of the International Battalion. For those of us who come from the front it means re-establishing contact with the outside world, and getting the latest news from America, France, and England. There I met Regler, Hemingway, Franklin, Ivens, and was proudly made to realise once more that the leading artists and intellectuals of the day have come to Madrid at the risk of their lives to attest their solidarity with our cause. Could Franco make a similar claim ? What of the writers on the reactionary side ? Has any Hans Heinz Ewers, Daudet, or Maurras taken service with the so-called Nationalist forces ?

LOS CHICQUETILLOS

THE CORPORAL CAME TO ME AND SAID THAT HE was damned if he was going to occupy the dangerous listening post with the support of only a set of kids—*chicquetillos* as he called them. I had a good look at the four raw recruits I had allotted to him that afternoon, and realized that he was right. Although they gave their ages as seventeen, they struck me as being nearer fifteen than sixteen. Usually at that age a Madrid boy is quite a man, but these were typical peasant lads with the faces and bodies of children. It almost looked as if they had borrowed their clumsy, gnarled, and weather-beaten hands from their fathers, at the same time as their trousers, which, though turned up, were still too long.

The cream is indeed off the milk, I said to myself. These boys are no longer like the volunteers who in September came to present themselves at barracks, in their dark red mufflers, and singing as they went, and whose eyes were burning with a mystical fanaticism born of the will to win. Although they had in their pockets a membership card of the youth association with only one stamp on it, they almost certainly belonged to the poorest of the poor, and had been sent to the front by their parents from some hungry village or other for the sake of the ten pesetas pay. I sensed, too, that political conviction could not have struck very deep roots in boys who had never seen the inside of a school and were ignorant of the alphabet. At the same time, I was aware that most of the others had not derived their socialism from books; that it had been acquired solely in the harsh school of hunger, injustice, and privation. However that might be, I distributed the boys over four different sections, where they found themselves in the company of our veterans from the Sierra, and I then had too many other things to worry about as captain of my company to think much more about them. We were lying at the time in the mud and dirt of some shallow trenches opposite Las Rosas. Water was oozing to such an extent out of the ground that even the straw in our dug-outs was soaked. From the Guadarrama Mountains an ice cold wind was blowing most of the time, and although no fighting of any importance was taking place, the well-directed bullets of the enemy were inflicting casualties upon us almost every day. With two bouts of sentry duty of three hours each and our continued shortage of men we were finding life particularly strenuous.

Apparently, however, my four *chicquetillos* did their duty. At any rate there were no complaints, and I was not called upon to take any disciplinary action. Quite by accident, I noticed upon one of my rounds that little Diogracias was on sentry duty with his bare feet in shoes that were too big for him ; either he thought this was the correct thing, or he was too shy to ask for socks.

Spring came. In the sheltered residential districts round Madrid, where I had gone on forty-eight hours leave to have myself measured for a uniform, the almond trees had long been in bloom and under the grave oaks of the Pardo the ground was purple and yellow with flowers. But the bare upland where we lay continued to be the same bleak wilderness where only the black contours of a few corpses were silhouetted against the brown mud in no-man's-land. All at once, however, as if acting upon revised orders, the wind dropped and from behind the clouds the sun shot out, bent upon making up for lost time. Two days later the whole bleak expanse had changed colour. Here and there yellow and purple flowers were peering through the young grass and along the stream that went meandering through the valley below, delicate willows had donned, almost challengingly, their yellow-green livery.

Mankind, too, seemed to awaken as from a winter

sleep. Energy returned with the sun and in the matter of military reorganization we made up within a few weeks for the neglect and lethargy of many months. From the booty captured at Guadalajara we received new Italian machine-guns. Steel helmets were distributed and military instruction was resumed. Food became more plentiful again and better than it had been for months ; it included the first oranges from Valencia, a very welcome addition to our diet. The wounded and the sick, now restored to health, returned in driblets from the hospitals to the front, and a few days later, owing to the recent levies, the company was up to strength. I now was able to devote more time and attention to the men themselves.

With the fine weather, they had crept like snails out of their shells. The sound of the flamencos was heard every evening. We set ourselves to work and in the course of a few nights we extended our trench by a few hundred metres in the direction of Las Rosas. But during the day, and more particularly during the holy hour of the siesta, when neither side was in the habit of shooting, we took sunbaths in the trench. The older members of the company had built a sort of shelter, thatched with foliage, which protruded above the parapet, and was a convenient target for enemy bullets. They went whizzing through the branches and beyond into the level stretch behind us. But beneath the willow foliage our men were sitting in quiet content on a small bench, telling each other endless stories, as was their wont on the village plaza. They also discussed the price of pigs and talked of the year 1925 when the corn stood so high in the fields. The younger men on the other hand were passing round portraits of their sweethearts or, with their tongues lolling, were writing letters of which they decorated the margin with coloured pencil drawings. But the fine weather had changed my four *chicquetillos* more than the rest. They were like frisking lambs led out to pasture for the first time, and their animal spirits were almost not to be kept within bounds.

Diogracias, who has a small belly and a mouth that always smiles, does sentry duty with nothing on except shoes much too big for him, white shorts, a steel helmet, and only a belt and gas mask hanging from his naked body. Agapito Salido has been indulging too freely in sun bathing, and his skin is peeling off like the bark of a plane tree. Pedro Nenni, who is not satisfied with the portrait I drew of him because it makes him look too much like a small monkey, is perpetually grinning with a sardonic smile which stretches from one low-hanging ear to the other. From the decorative point of view these recruits have not greatly added to the distinction of our new army ! But that is the least of our troubles. Unfortunately, the stimulating air of Spring is coursing like young wine through their veins. One moment I find Rubio walking on his hands, his large feet dangerously protruding above our breastwork, and the next I catch the four of them playing leap frog or turning somersaults and crashing through the roof of our shelter at the very feet of our grave and dignified sergeant, Florenciano. On such occasions there is no alternative but to punish them, and half an hour later I see a repentant Diogracias, busy with spade and pickaxe, while the others are enjoying their midday nap.

Of course, Florenciano is right : soldiers are soldiers irrespective of their age. Still, I am worried : if to-morrow the boy were hit by a stray bullet, how should I be able to answer for the fact that I have robbed his young life of even an hour's fun ?

Since then, however, I have discovered ways and means of canalising their excess of energy. The first of May is approaching and our commandant has ordered competitions in sprinting and jumping, and a few selected men from each company will be allowed to take part. Accordingly, I am busy every morning getting about a dozen volunteers into training.

We have chosen as our training ground the valley

on our right intersected by the stream. For a long time this valley was only a menace to us ; unseen the enemy could have crossed it in the night to attack us in the rear. A machine-gun in Las Rosas was trained directly upon the stream and made it impossible for us to dig a trench.

But now Spring has come and the thick foliage of the bushes along the stream has made us invisible. We can descend by a hollow path into the valley without being seen, and the enemy cannot afford to be so lavish with ammunition as to shoot without having a visible target. And so I am now giving gymnastic lessons every morning behind the fringe of bushes. Systematically I make them go through Müller's exercises and those I learnt in the camp of Noisy-le-Grand. The boys, who are all stripped, do their best as if I were giving them military instruction. During the intervals for rest, they paddle in the stream, bespattering each other with mud. It is remarkable how much more supple and agile they have already become in a few days. They derive much fun out of it, too ; in fact this hour's gymnastic lesson is for them the culminating point of the day. The enemy is entirely forgotten. Unfortunately, I know that the machine-gun in Las Rosas may begin to patter at any moment and that the leaves of the bushes offer no protection against bullets. I sometimes wonder if I am justified in what I am doing. It is certain that these bronzed bodies are now of much more use than they were, in the event of an attack, and the morale in the trenches is visibly improving every day. The boys are happy and, after all, a stray bullet might hit them anywhere. We are not sentimental and the words "quiza el camino hay que regar con sangre de la juventud"—maybe our path has to be sprinkled with the blood of youth—which everywhere else would be full of pathos, are here nothing but self-evident truth. And yet what would my feelings be if one day I had to carry back to the trench, bleeding and unconscious, one of these young bodies? . . . It is absolutely necessary that nobody should guess my thoughts, and I order: bend your knees, draw your breath as you rise!

The warm glittering sun of the Castilian tableland—so longed for during all these months—has only one drawback: the dead bodies in no-man's-land have begun to be malodorous. A sickly, sweet, oppressive smell is wafted on the tepid breezes and makes life in the trenches almost unbearable. Besides, the risk of typhus is anything but an imaginary danger. I felt compelled to ask for volunteers to help me bury the dead after nightfall. My four *chicquetillos* were the first to offer themselves, and, trusting to the temerity of youth that knows no danger, I decided to venture upon the job with them. That night, as luck would have it, the moon had momentarily disappeared behind the clouds. We slunk like cats out of our trench, and then crawled along the ground toward the hillside. Upon reaching the bottom of the valley, we were in the shadow and able to stand up and run along for a hundred metres or so. By this time the smell of dead bodies was noisome but it helped us to keep our sense of direction. Just as we were reaching the hill's edge on the other side, the moon appeared behind a cloud. I looked round and saw the four boys behind me standing motionless in the field. I felt bound to them by invisible threads; I knew that they had unlimited confidence in me, but also that they were without initiative of their own, and would be irrevocably lost if I did not keep my head. Again the moon buried its face in a cloud, and cautiously we crept along to where the bodies were lying—a grim, noisome mass in an advanced stage of decomposition. I had the greatest difficulty in repressing a sudden desire to vomit. Fortunately my boys had stronger nerves. Without giving further thought to the matter, they began hacking and digging, and within a few minutes the first corpse was buried. Meanwhile I surveyed the terrain. Thank goodness, there was a furrow near by which would afford protection in case of need.

Beside me the *chicquetillos* were stretching and bending down and their pickaxes hit the earth with a dull thud, giving off a small spark now and then when the iron struck the stone. Only one body was now left to bury ; in five minutes we would be returning.

At that moment a miserable stray dog began to yelp disconsolately somewhere in Las Rosas. My heart stood still : I ordered them in the furrow, but my mouth was as dry as dust, and I could scarcely bring out the words. Almost at the same moment a rocket went up and the ground around us lit up green. Two machine-guns began to patter angrily. We pressed our faces in the mud and heard the treacherous whistling of the bullets just above our heads. Apparently we had not been seen ; firing ceased after a good ten minutes. Our boys crept out of the furrow and, resuming their pickaxes, finished their work. We then proceeded on our way back. My revolver was weighing like lead in my hand. All the time I had to restrain myself from taking to my heels and running. The sensation of having the enemy at your back is far worse than when you go to meet him.

I had my morning coffee brought to me in my shelter and slept through the early hours of the morning. When I awoke the sun was blazing, and but for the sentries our trench seemed deserted. Whoever was not on duty had retired to the cool shadow of the dug-outs. Slowly I made my tour of inspection, and upon reaching the shelter where our *chicquetillos* were sleeping, I paused a moment. I heard a voice within stammering out the alphabet. I remembered that Carlos Suarez, our former book-keeper, who gave lessons to the illiterates, had told me that Pedro Nenni was among the best of his pupils. I brushed aside the sacking that was hanging at the entrance and crept inside. Suarez was sitting on his haunches and each of the four *chicquetillos* had a spelling-book on his knees. Pedro Nenni's mouth stretched open as far as his ears when he saw me. Trustingly he laid his hand upon my arm, and smiling said, " Aren't the Fascists bad shots ? They haven't learnt the use of the sights. That's why they always miss us. Their bullets fly too high."

PAJARO NEGRO (*The Black Bird*)

I CANNOT TELL FOR CERTAIN WHETHER IT WAS A magpie or a crow that our boys picked up somewhere among the bushes along the stream during those first spring days. What I do know is that the bird began by greatly resenting captivity, and showed it by ferociously pecking at the hands of its captor.

With a playful allusion to the Fascist aeroplanes, which were called " blackbirds " by our men, it was known as " nuestro pajaro negro." The boys were amused at the bird's still uncertain gait; pretending to let it go, they would catch it again with their caps when, too heavy for its young wings, it endeavoured to escape with a flutter and a jump. Within a few days, however, a quite different relationship was established between our pajaro negro and the men of the fourth company. The little bird's heart no longer beat so wildly and tumultuously against their horny hands and the crafty, beady eyes lost their expression of panic fear. In the trenches the boys vied with each other in their search for grasshoppers; noticing that their pajaro negro was scared by the perpetual twitching of these insects, they rammed their fat green bodies into its ever hungry, wide-open beak only after depriving them of their legs. At nights the bird slept warmly in the dug-outs half buried in the mops of the militiamen's unkempt hair. Our pajaro negro soon became the mascot of the company, and was shown to every stranger with much pride. Nevertheless, one fact was incontrovertible : the bird belonged to Juan Antonio who had picked it up. He, too, had taught it to march with little mincing steps to his word of command : " Left Right, one two, one two," and when Juan Antonio was on duty in the foremost trench, the bird sat on his shoulders. It seemed to have a dim awareness of what was happening, and had a particular aversion to machine-gun fire. When machine-guns began to patter on the other side it ruffled its feathers, looked sideways, and gave an angry, mischievous croak in the direction of the enemy—Kra, kra. If I happened to be passing by just then, Juan Antonio would stop me and say with a happy smile : " Can you hear, *teniente* ? It's saying *No pasaran, no pasaran.*"

This state of things lasted several weeks, and I have a strong suspicion that when Carlos Suarez was making up the list of the company in red and black ink with all the meticulous care which he was wont to use in his book-keeping days in Madrid, he also wrote down our pajaro negro, simply as militiaman number so and so. One morning I was giving my usual theoretical instruction to the men who were off duty in the second line. By then the sun was shining pitilessly and a number of the militiamen who had been on duty that night were only giving a drowsy look to the bullet trajectories that I was drawing on the company's blackboard. The arrival of the post was a welcome excuse for breaking off. Our comrades withdrew in groups towards their shelters. Whoever was able to read was never without a few mates, who peered over his shoulder and read with him, and whoever was innocent of the art had his letter read out to him word for word by the more scholarly comrades. No letter had come for me and I was sitting on a stone staring out in front of me a trifle sad and bored. I was startled out of my meditations by the rude sound of curses and abuse. Rows had been an extremely rare occurrence during the ten months we had already spent at the front, and it was therefore with amazement that I saw what looked like a scuffle outside the shelter at the farther end of the trench. I rose in haste and made for the scene of the disturbance; but already the men were moving up towards me and the little gipsy was in the vanguard carrying the dead body of our pajaro negro in his open hand. All he said was "assassinau" (murdered). From the confusion and excitement of voices all raised at once, I gathered that Juan Antonio himself had wrung the neck of his bird. I looked at him in astonishment ; he had been given a black eye, his hair was in disorder, and his face was covered in mud—the very image of a street urchin who had had a beating but who refused nevertheless to admit that he was in the wrong. All I could get out of him was, " With my bird I do as I like, and if I want to wring its neck, I wring its neck ; if they want to shoot me for it, let them go ahead."

The boys of the company were pressing round me, curious to know what I should say. I was more and more at a loss to know what to think, and wishing to gain time stooped down and picked up a crumpled sheet of notepaper that the wind had blown at my feet.

Automatically I smoothed out the sheets until suddenly I saw from the opening words that the letter was addressed to Juan Antonio. I then began to read attentively. It was a typical peasant's letter without capitals, commas, or full stops, full of grammatical errors in which the v's and b's were mixed up, the h's were absent wherever they belonged, and suddenly reappeared at unexpected places. I think I can remember its contents almost word for word : " dear juan antonio," his father wrote, " we are glad to hear that all is well with you and are pleased to let you know that all is well with me too and your little sister pepita is well too and so is carmen and your little brothers juanito and carlo and felipe and quintin are also doing fine and so are your friends pepe and antonio and so is your girl rosita and all of them greet you." Up to this point the letter was very clearly written. Then a couple of lines were scratched out as if the writer had hesitated what to write next. The letter continued, " and we regret to have to write that your mother is not so well because last week the blackbirds came over our village and bombed us and we all fled together in the fields, but your mother ran back to save the cow in the byre and when she got back to the field the blackbirds shot with their machine-guns and they hit your mother in the shoulder and your mother wants to know whether the captain would approve if you could come home for a few days on leave because she suffers great pain but that if it is not possible it is also all right because we are all suffering and struggling together for the cause (por la causa) and pepita and carmen and juanito and carlo and felipe wish to greet you and your friends too and also your girl and your father and mother embrace you and wish you all good luck from your father antonio."

When I had finished reading the letter I saw that Juan Antonio had turned away and was sobbing very gently, his face pressed against the breastwork. I said to the others, " Let him be, his mother has been wounded by the pajaros negros." They dispersed, and the little gipsy hurled the body of the blackbird over the breastwork in the direction of the enemy.

LA COSECHA ES SAGRADA (*The Harvest is Sacred*)

ONE DAY TACKS ITSELF ON TO ANOTHER—LIKE A chain-gang marching to eternity. Only, the sun grows fiercer every day and with the increasing heat the smell of unburied bodies, wafted to us by the wind, becomes more and more noisome. At the moment water constitutes our greatest problem. What we can get from the *noria* near our headquarters is warm long before it reaches the trench, and in the streams the water that is left here and there is muddy. Near the Casa del Cuartel there is still a pool where we are able to bathe ; its approach, however, is under enemy fire and we have made it a kind of sport to make a sudden dash and plunge before the machine-gun has time to go off ; the return journey has to be negotiated on our bellies through the dust.

In the valley about fifty metres in front of our lines I had discovered a sheltered spot where there was still some water. Its particular attraction was that it was not visited by horse flies, which have a way of settling on corpses. A few days ago I went and had my bathe there with Sergeant Adolf: suddenly we came under machine-gun fire. Adolf, who was lying on the spot where I usually take my sunbath, was shot in the thigh and in the shoulder. Once more I escaped scot-free. No wonder the boys joke about it, saying that Captain Last must have some guardian angel to protect him.

We now have our "hogar del combatiente" (soldiers' home) in the trench and a school where a "miliciano de la cultura" gives lessons with excellent results. It is a touching sight to see how the men who know their letters, but are not yet at home in spelling, get their brighter comrades slowly to spell out to them the letters they write to their families. A few days ago old Lopez came to me: it was absolutely necessary that the captain should read the first letter he had ever written. I read: "Dear Wife, I am happier every day that I came here, because here in the trenches I have learnt at last all the things I was never able to learn in our village."

One of our readiest pupils is little Pedro Nenni, but often he hasn't a mind for it and prefers to play truant when not on duty; then we see him hunting for lizards and serpents in the hills. I was not to be mollified by a small piece of roast lizard flesh which he offered me, but punished him with six hours extra sentry duty in the trench. A few days later the small bones of his right hand were crushed by a dum-dum bullet. When I visited him in the hospital of Valdelatas he let me see his bandaged hand, saying with a sad smile, " It hasn't helped, Captain ; now I won't be able to write, anyhow."

One of the most depressing tasks that devolve upon me as captain is to draw up the list of leave permits. Nobody knows when our company is to be relieved, and so long as this is the case I have only the right to allow two men on forty-eight hours leave to Madrid every three days. As our company numbers 140 men, it is not difficult to see what that means for those who are at the bottom of the list. Together with the political commissar I draw up the list as fairly as I can, bearing in mind such factors as the courage displayed by the men, their zeal, and their domestic circumstances, in so far as they are known to us. But special cases are always cropping up which make it necessary to effect some alteration. " Captain, my wife writes that she is likely to be confined this week."—" Captain, my mother is being evacuated to Valencia and would like to see me once more before she goes." Nearly always their requests are reasonable, often they are touching, and never yet has anybody tried to obtain leave in an unseemly or insolent manner whether in word or deed. But the others who are on the list have already been looking forward to going, and in most cases have already written home. Then negotiations have to be initiated and, after much talk and many sighs, he who is entitled to his leave usually renounces it voluntarily in favour of his comrade.

To make it somewhat easier for myself to maintain discipline I have introduced a uniform system of punishment. For venial offences I have a very simple punishment to which, however, they are strangely sensitive : I refuse to make a drawing of the delinquent. Their desire to have their portrait drawn is all the more remarkable because very few desire to possess it when it is finished. The great majority are quite content to be in my sketch-book, which they then expect I shall produce and show to anybody who is visiting the trench. Similarly, village children always ask to be photographed, though certain that they will never have an opportunity of seeing the result. Perhaps it is a vague, unconscious wish for immortality.

The other and heavier punishment I have introduced is to scratch out the soldier's name on the leave list and to place him at the bottom. When a few weeks ago Magro Vacas, one of my best sergeants, forgot the sentries in the front line when distributing morning coffee, I was compelled to show that the law applied without respect of persons to non-commissioned officers as well as to humbler fry. Vacas, who has a young wife in Madrid, implored me in vain to replace this punishment by any other, no matter how severe. You can well imagine that I was all the more elated when the order came through that all non-commissioned officers, whatever their place on the list, had to go to Madrid to have themselves measured for their new uniform. We happened to do the journey together. I scarcely had time to change at the Alianza when I was rung up by Vacas. "Captain, my brother is back too. In honour of this festive occasion we have killed a rabbit, and we should think it pleasant if you could join us." Needless to say I accepted the invitation. The table was set in a sort of veranda which lay in the shadow of fruit trees in bloom. Only the distant roar of the guns reminded us that we were at war. Sitting round the large flat dish out of which we all ate were Vacas, the parents, his wife, his brother, and a collection of little ragamuffins for whom eating apparently was such a serious matter that they forgot their native mischievousness. Now and then a spoon was planted in the middle of the dish as a sign that the wine was going round. Whoever then ventured to go on eating, before the spoon was removed, received a rap on the knuckles.

Suddenly, when conviviality was at its highest,

Vacas turned to his wife and said, pointing to me, " Look, Maria, here you have that cruel captain who begrudged my spending forty-eight hours with you." All eyes were upon me. Not unnaturally I flushed scarlet, saying awkwardly, " Now, now, you know yourself that you deserved your punishment," and Vacas as he got up to embrace me said, " But of course, Captain ; if I hadn't known that you had acted fairly, I would never have asked you here to partake of my rabbit."

During the November days, when we were holding the Estremadura road, I had realized the urgent need for a connecting trench between the two blocks of houses we were occupying. The work could only be carried out during the few hours between sunset and the rising of the moon. My men had been warned in advance, but when I came to fetch them one of them was just busy cleaning his rifle, another was warming his food, a third was sitting in his shirt hunting for lice and more than ten minutes had elapsed before I was able to get together a decent team.

" Ah ! well, off we go," they said at last, " if the *teniente* is so keen as all that . . . ! "

" Not because I am so keen, but because your own lives depend upon it ! "

They were amazed at my haste ; for them it could

all be done just as well *mañana.* Being a bit on edge, I went on to say : " You fellows are always singing, ' we shall win or die,' but when you are asked whether you would rather die or work, you prefer to die." This made them laugh, but once they were at work I had difficulty in getting them to break off before the moon rose.

Since then I have come to realize that what I once considered to be indicative of traditional Spanish laziness, was due more often than not to a lack of understanding of military necessity. How many hundreds of metres of trench haven't we dug this last month ! At the same time I remain convinced that the Spaniard makes no fetish of work ; he accepts it as a necessity, but will always prefer his siesta in the sun. Suddenly, however, my soldiers have a way of demanding work, and then it becomes a holy passion with them, rising up like a religious flame.

Spain is a peasant country ; even those soldiers, who have been living for years in towns, mostly came from the villages originally. Now, the carob beans had begun to ripen in the fields through which our trenches ran. Again and again I saw our men pulling out the yellowing plant and carefully weighing the small pods in their hard hands. Sometimes as I went by they offered me a handful of beans saying, " Taste them, they are getting hard already.

Within a week they must be carried off from the field, or the pods will burst open." Our commissar, who sensed what was brewing, came to me and said, " The boys insist that the harvest must not be lost on any account."

I thought it would be a good idea to promise a reward of a hundred pesetas for the platoon with the best record of work, but I very soon realized that it would be quite impossible to make a distinction between one group and another. They all set to work everywhere during every spare moment of their time, and automatically found their place in a long line of harvesters without having to receive orders from any sergeant or corporal. They got busy during the day in the valleys and the sheltered spots and at night in the hills ; they even worked through the sacred hours of the siesta while the sweat trickled down their naked bodies. Such was their fanatical zeal that a few groups actually ventured at night to gather in the harvest in no-man's-land right in front of our lines. I was just in time to prevent them from picking the carob beans which served as a very convenient natural camouflage for our nests of machine-guns.

During these activities two of my soldiers were wounded and one of my best men shot down ; but the work continued. The enemy must have wondered what was possessing us : our men never stopped singing for several days and nights. Finally, Fraigo Villarejo came to me and said, "We are through with the harvest, and the boys think that you had better give the hundred pesetas' reward to the school of illiterates for the purchase of books."

Yes, the harvest was over and everywhere the yellow stacks lay in the fields. But I had seen Montesino stumble and fall with outstretched arms, while from a small wound his blood was dripping on the carobs he had picked. Thank God, he had been shot in the heart and was dead at once. He was the most silent of our men, but also the strongest, the bravest, and the truest. Since he was not from Madrid, we buried him in the field where he had fought and harvested, and over his grave I read a poem from Miguel Hernandez :

The lads of fifteen and eighteen,
The lads of eighteen and of twenty,
They say : The firing line calls us,
We go to be made into men.
And should our last hour strike
Before we are grown into men,
Men we shall be in our graves.
If nothing is left of us, yet
Will the sun that we cared for shine on,
And our courage, a beacon for others.

In the mud and the slime of the trench,
In the chilly grey of the dawn,
In the heat of blazing midday,
We live our rebellious lives,
Rebellious to all subjection,
And a light illumines our ways
Until darkness encircles our bodies.
The dying are borne away
And their eyes are still ablaze,
Ablaze as if the morning sun
Were shining from their very eyes.

To the trenches they had gone
With resolution in their limbs
" Here we shall take root," they said.
" From here none shall uproot us."
And when Death came and reaped them,
Proudly he gazed on his harvest.
But in the shadowed lanes and alleys
They weep for them that fell,
Mothers who had given them milk,
Sisters who had cradled them,
Snow-white brides now decked in mourning,
Quivering, spent, and fever-blooded,
Peering over letters, portraits,
Weeping silently, uncomforted,
For all the beauty now departed.

Youth, sunny youth of Spain,
The fields are strewn with your bones,
And only the fame of your deeds
Endures and flows on like a brook.

Spill your blood in field and meadow
So that it turn to sap for olives,
So that your bones be turned to oak.
Blood that cares not to be spilt,
Youth that dare not offer it
Is not blood and is not youth,
And will neither sprout nor bloom.

Youth must needs press on, press forward,
Youth can never fail to conquer ;
All the perils of the future
Shall be met by Spanish youth.

The harvest was over but it had not yet been gathered in. On the horizon, behind the Sierra, leaden clouds were gathering. The stacks in the field were becoming yellower and yellower, and the soldiers said : " If the rain comes the pods will burst open and all our work will have been for nothing." At least a dozen times a day I telephoned to the " Comandancia," but always received the same answer. " Lorries cannot come out so far ; we have no carts and the mules that were promised us haven't yet arrived." Twice I sent our commissar to the Pardo, but in vain. The faces of my soldiers became graver every moment, and to make matters worse a fine drizzle began to fall towards evening. I sat in my shelter pouring out impotent curses on the heads of the Pardo authorities. Felipe came to warn me that a deputation of soldiers had arrived and wished to see me. Speaking in slow, measured tones old Lopez said :

" If the carob beans get damp and if then the sun comes out, the pods will break open and the harvest will be lost ; but if we all lend a hand we can carry it away in our blankets in one night to the spot where the cars can pick it up. The men want to know whether that's all right for you ? "

It was a heavy responsibility for me to take : the place where the cars stopped was more than a kilometre behind our line. I sent out a few patrols to make sure that all was quiet in the direction of the enemy. Had they attacked that night, they would have found ten men in the trench ; all the others were in the field, in groups of four, laboriously carrying off the carobs in their blankets. But the harvest was brought in.

ON LEAVE

June 15th, 1937.

IN ONE OF MY TALKS OVER RADIO MADRID, I SAID : " Everything is habit. The population of this city has grown accustomed to living heroically, as other peoples, alas ! are getting used to a life of cowardice from which they are perishing." More recent events have only increased my conviction that, generally speaking, courage is not congenital, but rather the result of habit or of a conjunction of certain circumstances.

There is the blind courage of those who have insufficient imagination to visualize danger, the courage of youth which is so full of vital force as to be unable to believe in its own death. There is the bull-fighters' courage of those who walk straight to their death so long as they know that the eyes of their comrades are fixed upon them, but who, if left alone at night at an advanced post, are suddenly seized with panic, and slink back trembling in every limb though no enemy may be in sight. There is the courage of the intellectual who knows how to dominate a deep, overpowering fear by conscious will-power.

There is also the courage of habit, which explains the miner's indifference when he reaches the danger zone in the shaft and the casualness of the soldier who ceases to bend down when the bullets begin to whizz past him. But more significant still is the enormous difference between moral and physical courage. I have often seen the bravest in battle tremble like a reed behind the front when reprimanded by his superiors. Seasoned revolutionaries have often subsequently shown themselves capable of every moral cowardice and every form of treachery to old friends, from fear of falling in disfavour with party headquarters. For myself, I never was one of those adventurers who like danger for danger's sake. Although I have never avoided danger where I considered it the unavoidable concomitant of my whole attitude to life, I had already as a boy a healthy dislike of scraps and an aversion to thin ice. On September 20, 1936, Harry D. and I arrived in Madrid. The following evening at 9 o'clock we were drafted in the Fifth Regiment, and at 11 o'clock we heard that our company would move forward that very night at 2 o'clock. In the bare room of the former monastery, an old party member who had taken part in the struggle of the Schutzbund in Vienna never ceased talking. I can still remember how I cursed him inwardly, and hoped that he would be silent a moment to enable me to overcome by a little concentration the fear within me that was gathering in intensity. A few days later—for in the meantime counter-orders had come in—when it actually came to going to the front, the fear of being afraid was what possessed me, the fear lest in battle I should cut a ridiculous figure in the presence of my comrades. But once in action this feeling disappeared entirely in the thrill and interest of the whole situation. I can remember, too, moments of real danger earlier in my life, when my intellectual activity and curiosity to know how events would shape themselves were such as to banish fear which usually only returned hours afterwards when all was quiet. Here in the field I can confidently say that I have never known fear. At Getafe and Villa Verde I acquired a reputation for unusual courage, although in the first of these two battles indignation was my predominant emotion, and in the second I was primarily animated by a sense of duty mixed with despair. Here in the trenches I am supposed to lack caution. The truth is, however, that I have usually too much to think about to remember to bend down when I find myself in exposed situations. But Felipe is my guardian angel. He brings me my steel helmet, which in moments of danger I am in the habit of forgetting, and on patrol he does not allow me to proceed until he himself has made a thorough survey of the next hundred metres. During the night preceding May Day, together with Felipe and Sergeant Vico Barneci, I planted a flag less than a hundred metres away from the enemy line without being conscious of any feeling beyond excitement and satisfaction.

And now at midday the commandant unexpectedly came to our trench with a few foreign officers, and said very casually, as if it meant nothing in particular, that during the coming night the company would have to make ready to be relieved.

The nerves of all the men were strained to breaking-point. We had become more or less reconciled to the idea of remaining in this mud until the end of the war, and the promise that we should be going for ten days to Madrid was too good to be true. For the first time in ten months I had two cases of drunkenness in the trenches. At 2 o'clock the fresh recruits who were to relieve us actually arrived. The first and then the second and third platoons gave up their weapons and marched off with their officers. For the last time I walked along the defences with the new officer in command. Suddenly upon signing the leave-book a great feeling of emptiness came over me now that I was deprived of the responsibility that had been mine for so many weeks. " Come along to company headquarters," I said to Felipe, " the others are already waiting there." I knew every inch of the road for having taken it regularly two or three times a day ; we were enveloped in darkness and the enemy was quiet.

As we were climbing out of the trench, a bullet came whistling over my head. At the same moment I was seized by an almost panic fear such as I had not known all these months. " Not now," the words went thudding through my head. " Not now, on these last five hundred metres, as I am about to go on leave." Only Felipe was walking beside me. I am sure that if he had not been there I would have covered the whole distance in one headlong dash. Only the thought that Felipe must on no account notice my fear held me back. When finally I reached headquarters, it was several minutes before I was able to give an order in a calm and controlled voice.

Happy, but tired and hungry with marching, we reached Madrid. Not until we had changed and been deloused and inoculated were we allowed to go home. Half dazed we looked at the trams going by and the traffic in the streets. I was wondering where I should get something to eat at that time of day, when Magro Vacas flung his arm around me and said, " Come along with me, I am certain my wife will have something in the cupboard." I protested, firmly convinced that his wife would certainly prefer to be alone with him for the first hour or so. But Vacas continued to insist, and I knew that a Spaniard is only too quickly offended when his spontaneous hospitality is refused. In one of the meaner streets of the centre, we climbed up a bleak stair that smelt of cats. " She will be speechless with surprise and beside herself with joy when she sees me," whispered Vacas on the doorstep. " Here we are," he said as he thrust open the door.

His reception was not what he expected.

His wife, who was sitting by the window sewing, bent her head lower over her needlework. " At last," was all she said. Vacas became boyishly embarrassed at her coolness ; he offered me a chair and began to talk at once to break the silence.

" I thought you would have been a little more pleased to see me, particularly as I was within a hair's breadth of never coming back at all. As I was conducting the new recruits who had come to relieve us towards Las Rosas, the commandant told us to take the low road along the Playa, which was quicker. Near the Cuesta de la Reina the Moors spotted us ; first machine-gun fire and then shrapnel. My boys dispersed on all sides, seeking cover. I had to go backwards and forwards like a clucking hen to get them together again. To their honour, I must say, not one of them ran back to Madrid, but it was a miracle that I was able to get them in the wood with only two wounded. Bullets were whistling through the branches . . ."

As if he had dealt her a blow, she jumped up from her chair. " And you dare tell me that! That's what you are proud of! That heroism of yours, that war of yours! And we sit alone here months on end . . . No letter, no post card . . . This war of yours, what's that to us? The women want peace!"

I was fidgeting on my chair, greatly embarrassed. " I think, Vacas, it would be better if I went."

He had already put on his cap. " We'll clear out together."

Before we had reached the door Maria had thrown away her knitting and, her arms flung about Vacas, was holding him back. " You must not take it badly, *compañero* captain! I know quite well that I have been talking a lot of nonsense, . . . that we didn't wish for war, . . . that the Fascists began it, . . . that there can be no peace till we have won. In fact, I told him myself he had to join up . . ." And turning to Vacas, " I know it was mean of me to say what I did, but you must not go away. . . . You were so long in coming and I was going mad with being alone. . . . And, my dear, if I was like that, it was only because I'm so terribly fond of you."

Vacas was now fondling and kissing her to calm her down. All his anger had departed and, proudly turning towards me, he said : " You see, that's how she is ; that's how she is when you look into her heart. The trouble is that she is already three months gone."

Maria raised a threatening finger at him. " Fie, must you go blabbing about that ? " She brushed away her tears and dashed towards the kitchen. " And now you will see all I have kept back for when you would be coming. Look at this, . . . and this, . . . saved up from the food distribution, . . . and this cheese from Uncle Angel when he came from the village." In no time the table was covered with a fantastic assortment of things : Russian preserves, fruit jelly, little cakes, bread, and even a small dish of margarine.

Vacas was clutching at his wife as she passed. " Maria, what a marvel you are ! "

She pushed him aside. " Just wait. If I can be sure that you two won't be running away, I'll just run up the street to tell Juan and Pedro that you are here. At the same time I shall get some wine . . . and "—now she assumed a mysterious air—" I know where cigars are still to be got."

Within half an hour it looked as if the whole

street had assembled in Vacas's room. Most of them had brought one thing and another along with them, and some of the women were helping Maria in the kitchen to bake some fish-cakes. The gramophone was turned on. It began by playing " hijos del pueblo," but very soon the company showed a marked preference for American fox-trots.

Pedro, with a bibulous glint in his eye, was thumping Vacas on the shoulder. " You can be proud of your wife," he was saying, " she keeps up the courage of the whole neighbourhood. The co-operative laundry for the battalion is her work too, and she is also district treasurer for the Red Help."

Meanwhile, I was trying to make a sketch of Vacas, who complacently posed for me, puffing at his cigar with obvious delight. Maria came out of the kitchen and peered critically over my shoulder. " It's like him," she said, " but you have flattered him terribly. All the same, it's very like what he was in his young days."

Vacas protested. " You wait a bit till I have shaved. You'll see, I'm still the handsomest man in the district."

Pedro took me by the arm. " I think it's about time we now left them to themselves ; we'll go to the *bodega* downstairs and drink to the coming victory."

But Vacas was never to see victory. Three days

after we had come back from our leave, he fell as we captured the vineyard.

About this time, I met with another experience. While I was the guest of the Fifteenth International Brigade, I made the acquaintance of a young Croat poet. We were returning from a children's party which had been organized in the village by the soldiers of the Chapaiev Battalion. The sultriness of the day was still hanging under the trees and from the direction of the village came the soft strains of a concertina. Now that the children's party was over, no doubt our soldiers were dancing there with the village lasses.

The poet was talking about a book he was busy writing ; its title was to be, " The Child that missed its Death." We went and sat by a stream, and he began to tell me how the idea of the book had come to him through the war.

During the Guadalajara battle he was suddenly buried under a heap of sand thrown up by the explosion of a heavy bomb dropped from an aeroplane. The first moments were entirely filled with anxiety and a terrifying sense of suffocation. " Suddenly," he said, " both fear and pain were gone. With an almost photographic realism I saw the faces of my comrades, of my mother and father ; I saw our village, the way that led to school, the sea at Valencia, and also Madrid, very small and very white as perceived from an aeroplane. I can see it all even now, and more clearly than what is actually surrounding us. Everything was suffused in a very peculiar light. Everything had an intensity and at the same time a sense of peace, of happiness even, which since then I have nowhere been able to find. After that, I must have become unconscious. But what I am driving at is this : from that day life has ceased to be a serious matter for me ; it has, if you can understand what I mean, become something gratuitous. I join in with the rest, I attack, I talk, I write, but the queer thing is I don't for a moment believe in it myself. There is no religion or mysticism in all this ; only the feeling that all the time I am living in a film. Now if you go to the pictures in Madrid, you come out again and find yourself standing in a street without lights. But that bomb seems to have carried me upwards and I have never since returned to terra firma. For me, the question that dominates all others is whether a child that has missed its death can ever again find its roots in life. I sometimes feel that a great injustice was perpetrated upon me when I came to be born for the second time and in the same circumstances of misery and pain."

No, as he describes it, I do not know the feeling.

I can remember two occasions in the course of this war when I felt conscious that all was over with me. Once at Vallecas and again not so long ago, when just behind me in the trench two men were literally smashed to bits by a shell. It is true that since then life has acquired a somewhat gratuitous quality ; it is as if an extra had been thrown in which one really no longer deserved. Life has consequently lost much of the seriousness which it must have for a good book-keeper or a station-master who sees to it that every train is on time. Since then, life has become more of a game, although even a game has its deliberately serious side and its unconstrained grace. For me it is not so much that the seriousness of life has been forfeited as that it has been thrust back ; it is as if behind the apparently important factors in life, I had discovered other, more real, bases for living. Perhaps life had lost its meaning for Stenko because he was still too young to know what it is to live. Perhaps he was one of the many who hesitate between fantasies and theories, without having known the ultimate realities, the warm breath of a mouth, the deep heart-beat under a human breast which alone give significance to life.

GOOD-BYE TO THE FOURTH COMPANY

July 1937.

YES, I MAY SAY THAT I WAS PROUD OF MY COMPANY the morning we again set out for the Pardo. They were supposed to report at 9 o'clock, and when the lorries were brought up at half-past nine the company was complete but for two men. In October, when our battalion had to move forward, buglers were careering the streets and sounding the assembly in front of every café. If the time fixed was 9 o'clock in the morning, one was only too glad to set out with about two-thirds of the company at about 11 o'clock at night. The others would come dribbling in a day or two later. This state of things has long ceased to be, although after long leave it is still usual for a company to be short of some twenty or thirty men on the first day on a number of pretexts. It goes without saying that the knowledge that all are present raises the morale of the company.

"Hullo, Domingo; hullo, Nicasio! And where have you two been?"

There is an exuberance of spirit as in the first

days of the war ; you would almost think the company were setting out for a picnic. There is singing all the way ; and the song of Captain Last, the text of which I cannot resist sending you, is added to the " International " and the " Red Flag " :

Los Holandeses preguntan
donde se encuentra Jef Last,
metido en una chabala
sin poder ni respirar.

Y los molinos de Holanda
giran, giran sin parar ;
preguntando con el viento :
donde se encuentra Jef Last ?

Y nosostros le decimos :
ganando la guerra esta
en el frente de Las Rosas
que le han hecho capitan.

And the Dutch, they go on asking
what can have happened to Jef Last,
lying secreted in a shelter
where it's not easy for him to breathe.

(This couplet can be repeated indefinitely by substituting the British, the French, the Germans, not to mention the Abyssinians, for the Dutch.)

And the windmills of his Holland
go grinding, grinding without pause ;
And turning to the winds they ask :
but what could have happened to our Jef Last ?

But we can tell them where he is :
he is here and winning the war
with us on the Las Rosas front
where they have made of him a captain.

From the other lorries they are drinking my health in bottles of Malaga wine, brought along from Madrid. Felipe, having somehow made his way through the throng, is now standing close beside me and endeavouring with a few words to show his attachment to me. " Captain, mother has given me a bottle of olive oil. When we reach the trenches my first business will be to clean your revolver and stand it in the oil."

Yes, I am proud of my company this morning, proud and happy. It has been my work ; it is worth more to me than any of the books I have ever written. It is not only a military unit, and a jolly good one, it is also a community of friends, a fragment of socialism in action—the socialism for which I have lived.

Harry Domela, who is now on the staff, doing excellent survey work and also directing operations, was waiting for me to show us our new positions. What he had to tell me was not very enlivening news. Since Manolo Fernandez was promoted from battalion commander to brigadier, a change has come over him which is anything but to his advantage. His devotion, his courage, and his working capacities continue to be unquestioned. His psychological insight is remarkable, and he has a natural outstanding aptitude for military tactics. His memory, which is astounding, is the repository for all the data concerning the men, armament, and ammunition, which alas! are not to be found in a single document of the brigade headquarters staff. For, above all things, Manolo is distrustful. He is suspicious of treason, which may lurk anywhere, but his supiciousness arises also from a highly developed inferiority-complex. He is entirely self-taught and has many gaps in his education. To prevent possible robberies from taking place in the quartermaster's stores, he would like to be able to tap out the lists of boots on the typewriter himself! Indeed, he is sometimes busy for hours slowly groping his way on the keyboard of the machine. He cannot bear the thought of not being able to master the instrument. On the other hand, a military or theoretical handbook is nowhere to be found in his office. He senses that the help of the intellectually trained is necessary to him, but his feeling for them is a blend of distrust and contempt. Where were the intellectuals in the days when he had to fill his hand-grenades himself with dynamite? The intellectuals already know too much about things; now, curse them, they seem to be trying to steal a march upon him. While ever ready to use the intellectuals for his own purposes, he will be equally ready to kick them down immediately afterwards from fear of being superseded by them. Thus it went with Diego and with Cavada's brother-in-law. Now Harry is being threatened with the same fate.

According to Harry, there is no plan, however perfect, which Manolo will not change at the last moment. Nearly always it is a change for the worse, but he has to show that he is not just prepared to take on other people's plans. Since Malaga, but especially since the events in Barcelona, Manolo's distrust has assumed morbid proportions. Of party policy he knows little more than what he has read in a few pamphlets and in yesterday's *Mundo Obrero*, and for this very reason he is inclined to see *saboteurs* and traitors everywhere.

Since the party in Madrid disseminated the rumour that I was a Trotskyist, Manolo's distrust is primarily centred upon me and also upon Domela for going about with me. Diego has warned me never to leave the trench without my orderly, and now Domela has also been telling me of Manolo's threatening words when he talks about me.

Since Harry left me, I have been sitting in the dark thinking things out. It is clear that Manolo's refusal to give me leave to attend the writers' congress also proves there is something wrong. One gets a little weary of these accursed suspicions of Trotskyism. As a matter of fact, I am convinced that, since October at any rate, Trotskyism in Barcelona is on the wrong track. It has been trying to pursue a revolutionary course at a time when—no matter through whose fault—such a course had long since lost all possibility of succeeding. Fundamentally I agree with my men when they say that perhaps the Trotskyists have been provoked but that one should not allow oneself to be provoked to such lengths.

Certainly, Manolo understands human nature; but he does not know me well enough Although I have always spoken well of the Soviet Union, he feels instinctively that my enthusiasm is luke-warm. At the same time he is wrong when he imagines that I should ever let that appear in front of the soldiers. Since my visit to Russia in 1936 and since the trials, I know that there is nothing more to be expected from that quarter from the socialist point of view; but I know too what Russia means to our soldiers here at the front. The so-called Democracies have betrayed Spanish democracy. The Second International does philanthropical work by sending warm underclothing and setting up hospitals. The leaders of the international trade union movement have not had the courage even to declare a one-day strike. We are completely left in the lurch and desperate ; only two bright spots remain on the horizon : Mexico and Russia. Mexico can send rifles but no tanks or guns. Russia has provided effective help. Whether it came soon enough, whether it was adequate, and whether it can be compared with the assistance afforded by the Fascist countries to Franco, are other questions. For the time being Russia is our one hope, our only ally. Without Russia we should have been lost long ago. Whoever attacks his one ally in the midst of the struggle is stabbing his own troops in the back. If only Manolo could peer a little deeper into my heart, he would know that my one and only desire is to go on struggling with this company of mine unto death or to victory, without any thought of dabbling in politics.

The order to occupy the vineyard in no-man's-land was greeted by our men with general approval. It had long been a sore point with them that the grapes which we could already see with the naked eye should be allowed to wither on their stems this Autumn or fall into the hands of the Fascists. There was, besides, little danger attached to the operation ; it was a question of occupying quickly and unexpectedly the next ridge and of digging oneself in before daylight returned. All in all, it cost us the life of one man and one wounded, no more than what we might have lost on any day. The company was expecting a reward ; instead of which, it had to submit to reorganization, and within a week we were all scattered and broken up. All my six sergeants were replaced by others, and I lost my most trusted soldiers to other companies. When I made a complaint I was told that these men had to contribute towards raising the morale of the newly-formed companies of fresh recruits. That sounded plausible in the case of an experienced soldier like Vico Baruecci ; but how, in heaven's name, could this apply to the *chicquetillos*, for instance ? Francisco Fraijo said openly what was in the minds of most : " Manolo is evilly disposed towards you and wants to isolate you." To make matters worse some of the new-comers here are definitely inferior specimens of humanity. Machado, for instance, had to be placed under arrest for drunkenness the very first day. Lopez's pocket-book has been stolen from his dug-out and, in spite of thorough investigations, we have not been able to trace the money. Now Faustino and Felipe, whom I had recommended for the officers' college, are also going away. In a fit of depression I asked to be transferred to another brigade. My application had a surprising effect. I was summoned to headquarters that very night and informed that my transfer had already been decided upon. According to a new ministerial decree all foreigners have to be drafted into the International Brigade : " If you please, Don José, here is your travelling pass for Albacete." I scarcely had time to haul my belongings out of the trench and to shake hands hastily with some of the comrades. Manolo's last word explained it all : " It will be easier to supervise you out there." I then presented myself at divisional headquarters in the Pardo, where I was received in the friendliest manner. Cavada, who meanwhile has become colonel, regrets my departure, and in his own hand has written a letter of recommendation, and a sort of testimonial to the effect that he is very satisfied with me, not only on grounds of courage, but with regard to my work as a captain. A staff car took me to Madrid. Before reporting at the base of the International Brigade, I hurried along to the Alianza to collect some of my things. In my room I found a note from Maria Teresa, informing me that I had received a permit for the writers' congress and could obtain a travelling pass from Miaja. This note is three days old ; apparently it was held back by Manolo. Upon whose orders ?

ANTI-FASCIST WRITERS

As THE CAR WITH THE OTHER OFFICER WRITERS (Renn, Bodo Uhse, Kantorovich, Bates) had already left a few days before, I took the motor-bus-train connection via Tembleque and Albacete. There is no sadder spectacle than a charabanc full of evacuated people. When you see the careworn, emaciated faces of the women, their miserable baggage, the little ones whining with fatigue and hunger, and the proud stoical silence of their older brothers, you are suddenly made to realize why so many prefer to remain in Madrid in spite of the bombardments and recoil from undertaking a journey into the unknown and without any certainty that the refuge they are seeking will not be bombarded too.

The train, which was already three hours late at Tembleque, was held up at every halt. The four hundred kilometres separating us from Valencia were covered in about twenty-seven hours. What struck me was the excellent condition of the rolling stock. Not a window-pane was missing from the carriage-doors. Every seat had its leather cushion ; nor were any names scratched upon the wood by way of souvenir. To-morrow these carriages will again be able to serve for the international tourist traffic without having to be overhauled. There was even a restaurant-car attached to the train, where unfortunately there was nothing to be got except unripe fruit, Malaga wine, and coffee without milk or sugar. In the train I shared my compartment with a few young, particularly attractive Spanish officers. They had taken part in the struggle around Malaga to the bitter end.

" Betrayal there may have been," said one of them, " but no breath of suspicion attaches to the soldiers. They held out to the very last ; unfortunately we had scarcely any machine-guns . . ."

" And no guns at all," said the second.

" Nor were there any tanks," added the third, " and the Italians arrived with their fully motorized columns."

All was silent. After a few moments the lieutenant went on : " When all was lost we marched for seventy-eight hours through the mountains without a break. We could not rely entirely upon the peasants, because many of them were embittered by the measures of compulsory collectivization enforced by the Anarchists in that province. An uninterrupted stream of hundreds of thousands of refugees endeavoured to reach Almeria. The bridge at Motril had been washed away, and our soldiers stood in the water for hours at a time helping the women and children to cross over. . . . There I saw workers who in their despair shot down their own wives and children with a revolver . . ."

I was reminded of the Dantesque accounts of Doctor Bethume (of blood transfusion fame), on the subject of this flight, which constituted the most tragic plebiscite ever declared against Franco. " They were bombed from the air and shelled from the mountains by the artillery ; and from the sea by the cruisers of non-intervention. Not a vehicle was to be found on those two hundred kilometres of road ; no water, no food . . ."

" Many prisoners ? " I asked.

" Thousands," said the lieutenant.

" What happened to them ? "

" I will tell you," said the *alvarez*, bending closer towards me, " One night, not a month ago, we were stationed on the Jarama. Three deserters crossed over to us ; boys from Malaga. They told us that the captured battalions were deployed in rows of single file. Every fifth man had to step out to be shot. ' That was the most awful experience of all,' they said, ' to be standing there without being allowed to look to the right or to the left, and not to know whether you were number two, three or five, and the counting lasted for hours . . .' When they had witnessed the shooting down of one-fifth of their comrades, they were given the choice between being shot down as well and fighting in the foreign legion on Franco's side. Most of them chose the second alternative, thinking that once they were at the front again they would be able to desert. This was precisely what these three had done, and they told us that the following evening a great many more would probably arrive. None came, however, neither that evening nor the next, and it was more than a week before eleven more deserters suddenly crossed over to us. We asked them why there were so few and why they had not come sooner. Then they said, 'The morning after the first three had deserted, the officers shot down all the sentries who had been on duty that night. They also gave out that, if there should be any more desertions, not a single man from Malaga would be left alive in the battalion. That was why we hesitated, but when yesterday evening we heard your loud speaker and knew that there were men from Malaga here too, we could no longer hold out and we came, although we know that it means death for the others.' "

The bomb-shattered hall of the town council of Valencia. The meeting was opened by Negrin, the

Prime Minister, who withdrew immediately afterwards, and grey-haired Anderson-Nexö took the chair. In letters of gold the names of our honoured dead stood out in the hall : Garcia Lorca, Valle Inclan, Ralph Fox, General Luckasz . . .

Our comrades Prados and Regler were lying gravely wounded in hospital. Many of those present were front-line soldiers—Malraux, Renn, Bates, Uhse, Kantorovich, Alberti, Paraguas, Duran. Cordoba Uturburi had been travelling from front to front, inspiring the soldiers to courage ; in the thick of the war Josephine Herbst and John dos Passos had visited Madrid in danger ; Koestler had been arrested at Malaga.

And now they were here, while only that morning the sirens gave warning of yet another air raid : Dr. Brouwer, Jean Richard Bloch, Leon Felipe, Champsom, Ehrenburg, Kisch, Nordahl Grieg, Anna Seghers, Huidobro ; writers from Spain, China, Chile, Iceland, France, Germany, England, Holland. In the background, sitting beside the austere Marchwitza, I caught sight of the smiling faces of Karl Bredel and Erich Weinert, who had come to join the International Brigade when the congress was over.

Whoever considers this list of names will realize that not a single bourgeois journalist would be likely to report upon this congress for his newspaper. But it is not difficult to imagine the cry of jubilation that would go up if a single scientist of the calibre of Hodan, a single humanist of Bergamin's distinction, could be reported on the side of Franco! Indeed, it may be asked how there could be such names in the ranks of those who stupidly shot down even the tender García Lorca, and who flash out their Browning when the word culture is so much as mentioned.

Literature is not to be made with lies, and no Fascist writer would venture to tell the truth on the subject of the prisoners of Malaga or the voluntary character of the Italian troops. It is no accident that the writers' congress for the defence of civilization should be held this year in Madrid. . . .

Before dealing with the congress itself, I should like to touch upon a painful subject. Without exception all the writers who have come here are brave men and women. They have had a surfeit of the false coinage that distinquishes words from deeds and they have stepped out of their ivory towers to hold the fort for civilization, and if necessary at the cost of their own lives. And yet . . .

It is good that the congress should have indicted the murder of Mühsam, the incarceration of Ossietzky, and espoused the cause of all the great writers who have been exiled from the Fascist countries or have lost their civic rights. But in the course of the proceedings other names were not so much as mentioned ; such names as Ottwald, Günther, Tarassov, Rodianov, Rom, Mandelstam, Tretiakov, Bezunienski, Jossiensky, Gronski, Kliuiev? Why ?

Why this conspiracy of silence around the cultural reaction in Russia, about which we are all agreed in private ? When we heard in Madrid that yet another school had been bombed, Kisch remarked : " When you hear of such horrors, when you realize what our enemies are, then your courage returns and again you feel inclined to defend everything that has been done on our side, *even the trials* ! "

But does this argument really clinch the matter ?

It might be alleged that conditions in Russia were here irrelevant, that what mattered was the defence of Spain, and that everything that was liable to impair this defence had to be avoided. This was Bergamin's point of view. At the same time it must be recorded that already at Valencia, the Russian delegation, which again included the ominous Bola, began by upsetting even the Spaniards by their entirely gratuitous attack upon the Trotskyists. From that moment it was clearly the main object of the Russian delegation to get some sort of motion carried against André Gide. Naturally I came to find myself in the very centre of these intrigues. From all sides (except the Spanish) I was approached, pulled about, and badgered. In these circumstances, it was difficult for me to express my full meaning although I already had done so in January in an article for the *De Kroniek voor Kunst en Kultuur*, which, through no fault of my own, though fortunately for me, was not printed. However, the speech I made was clear enough for any understanding person, and consequently was not published in the congress report of *Das Wort*, and only in a garbled form in *Commune*. Its full text appeared only in *La Hora de España*.

Subsequently the Russians endeavoured to have the motion introduced by the Argentine delegation. Supported by two eminent French writers, I protested against this attempt on the simple ground that the books of André Gide had not yet been translated in Spanish and could not be obtained anywhere in Madrid. It seemed to me a foolish procedure to expect this congress to sit in judgment over books with which the majority of its members were unacquainted. The Committee were of the same opinion, and the Russians had to be content with a personal declaration from Bergamin which was not further discussed.

I can only say again with all the emphasis at my

command that my defence of André Gide's criticism of Russia—which was morally brave and objectively necessary—did not imply that I agree with every aspect of his book. Furthermore I considered the publication of *Retour de l'URSS* at the time when it occurred as inopportune, and the book itself as dangerously one-sided. Whoever denies or minimizes the positive results of the Russian revolution—which can never be entirely undone, even by Stalin—throws away the good with the bad and risks infecting the working class with the mood of Madam Angot : " Ça ne valait pas la peine, vraiment, de changer de gouvernement."

It should never be forgotten that in Russia, for the first time in history, an interest in art and literature had been aroused among a whole people. I have seldom been so impressed as by the 1934 Congress of Soviet Writers in Moscow. From a human standpoint the speeches of Red soldiers and underground workers, of peasant women from the Kolkhosi farms and representatives of the youth movement, were often almost as important as the elaborate revolutionary reports of Bukharin and Radek. It was also the first occasion when an almost passionate interest was evinced by both writers and general public in their contacts with one another.

What took place in Russia then is now being

repeated in Spain. There is the same sudden craving for reading, which has made the selling of second-hand books in the streets of Madrid the most lucrative of all trades. Here too, circulating libraries are being installed in every town, in every village with a garrison, and in every trench. Here too, throughout the press, interest in the congress is so great as to overshadow even the military operations on the various fronts. Here too, the writers are not just among themselves: factory girls, boys of the Alerta, university students, and militiamen take part in the discussions. Soldiers were showing us the banners captured at Brunete, at the same time as the stolen feminine trinkets that had been found on a Fascist officer. The words of their leader, "We are writing history with these bayonets," was no empty phrase.

The writers' congress in Madrid was, also from the technical point of view, better organized than any I ever attended. A staff of young enthusiastic artists performed miracles, the full significance of which can only be understood by somebody who has lived in Spain during the war. The waiters' trade union and the town council of Madrid made it a point of honour to make such arrangements as to prevent their foreign guests from noticing any difference in the standard of living between Paris and Madrid. The translations were done with unexampled care. When I expressed my admiration for the fact that already the following morning the reports were at the disposal of members and duplicated in four languages, one of the young students in the office simply replied : " That's only because we've worked through the night." It was also an impressive performance on the part of our hosts that they were able to maintain an atmosphere of true culture in the very thick of the bombardments. The somewhat self-conscious advertising air of Russian congresses was tempered here by good taste rooted in centuries of tradition. The floral decorations of the hall were exquisite in every detail, and nobody is likely to forget the magnificently lyrical and stylized performance of Garcia Lorca's play, *Maria Pineda*, the concert where young composers conducted their own works, and the grand performance of the front marionette theatre at the Alianza. Dignity and grace presided over all.

Speech delivered in Madrid at the International Congress of Writers for the defence of civilization against war and Fascism.

COMRADES,—

There was a time when I hated Fascism with what I might describe as an intellectual hatred. All I knew of its teaching and its deeds, all I had read in books, and been told by comrades, struck me as not only repulsive but also as the very negation of our conceptions of civilization and life. I felt that it was better to die than to have to live under such a system, better to leave wife and children behind and come to Spain than to have to witness the poisoning of my children's minds which would inevitably result from the triumph of Fascism in Europe.

This hatred, comrades, which was an artist's hatred of ugliness, an intellectual's hatred of stupidity and lies, a human being's hatred of bestial cruelty—this hatred was already deep-rooted, but I must admit that now, after nine months of struggle in Spain, its character has changed entirely.

It is no longer intellectual ; it has gone over into my blood. It is an integral part of my being just as it has taken root in the very vitals of my noble companions, with whom I am fortunate enough to be allowed to struggle, shoulder to shoulder, in the same trench.

It is one thing to listen to what others have to say and to look at photographs. It is another thing to touch with one's own hands the mutilated body of a woman one has revered, to dig up the dismembered fragments of children who once played at your side, or to return to find in ruins the humble house where you were once a guest.

The totalitarian war, which is being waged against us, not only exceeds in cruelty, brutality, and cowardice everything the world has ever seen, but it also leaves far behind the most perverted and cruel fantasies of mankind. After all we have seen, we can no longer be impressed by the imaginative powers of an Octave Mirbeau, an Edgar A. Poe. A Dutch proverb says that one gets used to everything, even to hanging, and it is a fact that the Spanish people, and more particularly the people of Madrid, have grown accustomed to living in heroism, whereas other nations, alas ! are more and more developing the habit of living in cowardice. Your coming here has been a symbolical act, a proof of courage, an expression of faith in our victory, a gesture of alliance with the proletariat under arms. But it seems to me that your coming here is also important from another point of view.

If our struggle had only been a negative struggle against a certain thing ; if it had not also been—as our soldiers see it—a positive struggle for increasing the sum of love and righteousness in the world, for more freedom and more civilization, then this struggle would have been lost in advance.

What unites us here to-night is the struggle for civilization.

The one-time illiterate soldier in my company, who in his first letter to his wife, wrote : " I feel happier every day that I came here because in the trenches I have learnt everything I was unable to learn in the village," ; the soldiers who post up mis-spelt notices in the buildings of the University City, saying, " Comrades, do not touch these instruments, they serve the cause of science " ; the militiamen who at the risk of their own lives have saved works of art from the burning palace of the Duke of Alba—all these are defending the civilization that we are defending, a civilization they revere without ever having tasted of its fruits.

In his book on Don Quixote and Sancho, Miguel de Unamumo says that of the two figures Sancho Panza was the true idealist because he believed in Don Quixote. Certainly, one cannot read the masterpiece of Cervantes without noting on every page the reverence aroused in the plain man of the people by his master according to the spirit. Sometimes his veneration induces him to follow the intellectual even when with his sober peasant horse sense he realizes the foolishness of Don Quixote's words.

Far be it from me to set up a comparison between the proudly conscious and heroic Spanish people of these days and the Sancho Panza who, without defending himself, took all the blows, merely in the hope of acquiring his famous island. Such a comparison would be more apposite in the case of the Catholic peasant of the old days who was given the consolations of a hereafter. I venture to maintain, however, that in the integrity, courage, and righteousness of Governor Sancho all the essential characteristics of our brave soldiers are already to be found. Cervantes knew that when the proletariat assume the burdens of responsibility upon their own shoulders, they grow in stature and can rule more effectively than any duke.

Other writers have compared Don Quixote to the intellectual of the present day. Such a comparison lays an enormous responsibility upon us. If it be true that writers, according to Stalin's famous words, are the engineers of the soul, then we must exact from ourselves a quality of mathematical precision if we are to live up to this definition.

"Vigilance, vigilance, and still more vigilance," is another of our great leader Stalin's watchwords. Sometimes a doctor who is combating an epidemic is the first to become infected with the bacilli of the disease. Let us guard against all contamination. We have had enough of what a French writer has called "la trahison des clercs"; enough of mechanical proceedings and of the complacency of labels. Our purpose must never be merely to follow in the footsteps of journalists and orators. We have our own clearly defined duty: to deepen the significance of the Homeric struggle in which to our honour and joy we are allowed to take part. Let it not be said of us that moral courage is more difficult of attainment than the physical courage of the soldiers in the trenches.

It should never be forgotten that the basis of all civilization is criticism, including that self-criticism which Lenin never ceased to enjoin upon us. Where criticism is lacking, injustices grow and begin to fester like unattended wounds. They require to be lanced in order to be cured. Whoever maintains silence lest the enemy should turn his criticism into a weapon against us will sooner or later suffer the bitter experience of seeing abuses steadily growing by his very silence until these abuses speak louder than the word of any critic. The patient's life is threatened by the disease, not by the diagnosis of the doctor.

But I was speaking of deepening the significance of the struggle.

With all my heart I welcome the popular front that unites us in our struggle for democracy. I see in this popular front not only the guarantee of victory but the realization of one of the first wishes of the proletariat, and the first step on the road leading to the fulfilment of Marx's watchword : "Proletarians of all nations, unite."

There are times, however, when I feel that this popular front still assumes a too purely opportunist character. We must not leave matters as they are. Closer bonds than temporary expediency unite us to friends such as our chairman José Bergamin and to the heroic Catholic defenders of the Basque country. Marx's reference to religion as the opium of the people will not do ; it does not explain the genuine sympathy with which an ever-increasing portion of the Catholic youth come out to meet us. It is the intelligentsia's duty to probe into the factors that unite us ; not by congresses, but by going back to St. Francis of Assisi, to the Fathers of the Church, and to the religious socialists of the Middle Ages who were persecuted in the name of the same creed against which Hitler at this moment is taking up arms.

And there is another factor we must realize : the struggle of the proletariat is a struggle for the happier existence of future generations. The intellectuals must fight for the same purpose. Merciless war must be declared against all that remains of a bourgeois, capitalistic, or ascetic ethics, which is standing in the way of this happiness. The proletariat have the right to expect from us the foundations of a new ethics and a new art, in conformity with their requirements. Once liberated the eagle never returns to its cage. The modern Don Quixote must not be allowed to rest content in exploiting Sancho Panza for his own purely personal glory.

He must unite with the very soul of the people for the satisfaction of requirements that have been sanctified by so much human blood.

The struggle of the Spanish people is the struggle of the world proletariat for freedom, justice, and civilization. There have been moments when it has seemed to me a desperate venture. But in such moments I recall to my mind that other struggle which was waged by my own people against the proudest monarchy in the world, allied to an omnipotent church. I recall the year 1572 when the burden of the struggle was borne by only two of the seven provinces, when the regular army was destroyed, and when only the people in arms were defending what still remained of the free cities. All of you know the issue of this struggle. A few years later the liberated Netherlands entered upon their golden age ; in the arts and the sciences all the autocratically governed countries were outstripped. The struggle of our Beggars, the French Revolution, the glorious revolution in Russia are only episodes in the evolution of mankind. No stream ever returns to its source. The stream of human evolution has its source in the murky, blood-stained, fanatical past which the Fascists of to-day would like to re-instate. Evolution flows towards the untrammelled sea where " the International will be the human race." All honour to the Spanish people for being the first to break the dykes with which it was endeavoured to hold up this stream and for saving Europe from being transformed into a swamp in which every shoot of human civilization must needs be stifled. Honour and victory to my comrades in the trenches, who with their blood are writing nobler pages in the book of history than any that we shall ever write.

WE FORGE AN ARMY

August 1937.

"DE FRENTE, MAR!" (FORWARD; MARCH!)

"Izquierda, derecha, un, dos." (Left, right, one, two.)

From five in the morning till the beating of the tattoo at ten o'clock at night, orders echo through the village.

In the railway stations the Anarchists have posted up notices with the words: "Don't give military toys to your children." But at Madrigueras every child that is able to walk imitates the marching troops and plays at being a soldier.

"De frente, mar!" (Forward march!)
"Media volta!" (Right incline!)
"Paso ligero!" (Double!)

Who would have thought in those November days of last year that the Spanish people would have been able to overcome their natural inclinations to the extent of accepting this super-Prussian drill, and a routine in which merely to be three minutes late is considered a major offence? Who would have thought it possible that this dicipline could be imposed upon Catalans, who as recently as last June would not allow themselves to be drilled in barracks?

There can be no doubt, however, that the overwhelming majority of our boys are conscious of the absolute necessity of this discipline, and participate in military training with the greatest possible zeal. I never cease to rejoice at the freedom and keenness with which they come forward to have explained to them afresh what was not quite clear to them. Not an hour, literally not a minute, is lost while they are being trained. When towards evening I enter barracks, I repeatedly observe how they practise together the movements I have taught them during the day. And yet the service is incredibly hard under this broiling Castilian sun, and more especially in these waterless hills where the dust penetrates into every pore of your skin until you feel as if your whole body had become an American vacuum cleaner. Nevertheless, our men go creeping along indefatigably from vine to vine; nobody complains, nobody now knows what shirking means. I remember my own period of service in Holland and note with satisfaction that we have accomplished more in three weeks than used to be attained in six months.

There are a number of reasons for so much

spontaneous zeal. First of all, these Catalan recruits are nothing like as black as they have been painted. The great majority of them are not boys who have been pressed into service ; they are fighters who already heard the bullets whizz past their ears in the July days or later during the first offensive in Aragon. Among them are militiamen who set out with the first Thaelman column at a time when they had only one revolver and one rifle for every fifteen men, and had to capture the remainder of their weapons from the Fascists at Pina. Furthermore, everybody knows that the officers who have risen from the ranks are no *señoritos* and that they have to work far longer and harder than the soldiers themselves. Only when field exercises are over—and we ourselves first carry them out in every detail—do our real duties begin : officers' meetings, theoretical instruction, and preparations for the next day. I seldom get to bed before half-past eleven.

We are lucky, too, in having Heinz as our commandant, who is the admiration of all of us. He is a fine fellow and indefatigable. He it was who on the Jarama carried a wounded comrade for two hours on his back and brought him to safety, right through the enemy fire.

At the same time I do not deny that there is danger in a too rigorous enforcement of discipline such as is sometimes practised, especially by some of the younger German officers. Severe friction often arises between Dutch volunteers and their instructors. Dutch lack of discipline is not entirely to blame. The German lack of a sense of humour and of psychological insight is equally responsible.

Obviously all this may become dangerous, because no army in the world is exclusively composed of angels. Far the greater portion of our brigade consists of volunteers whose motives for coming here are purely idealistic. This is not to say that their idealism and their powers of nervous endurance will be proof in all cases against the baptism of fire. Some elements, and they are a tiny minority, become demoralized after a few months at the front. And of course it has been quite impossible in spite of careful sifting to avoid altogether a small percentage of adventurers and other unfortunate elements.

The letter which the Dutch political commissar received from one of the recent recruits at Pozo Rubio may be worth quoting in this connection.

Dear Sir,—

As you wish to obtain from us new-comers particulars of our former life, the undersigned with all due respect wishes to inform you of the following. His early youth was spent in the pick-pocketing profession. He had already acquired a certain proficency in the trade when the police put an end to his career by having him removed to a state institution. His ideal in those days was to become a gangster, but bitter experience taught him that Holland was too small and restricted a country to offer any real prospects. He thought burgling a dangerous occupation and took to coining instead, until the gilt was off the gingerbread here too owing to the devaluation. The undersigned is a Catholic and, as only Catholic papers came into his father's house, he got the impression that Red Spain had now become the ideal country for plunder and robbery. He therefore did not hesitate to join up as a volunteer. To his amazement, however, he landed in a training camp on the heath, where there is nothing to pinch or steal, where on the contrary he and his mates have to sweat for hours in the dust. The undersigned entreats you, dear Sir, to believe that nothing was further from his intentions. He begs you therefore to consider his having taken service as a mistake, and demands to be sent back to Holland, failing which other measures will have to be taken.

Yours respectfully,
P.C.

Naturally this request was immediately granted, and it is probable that the writer of the letter is one of those whose literary contributions were eagerly accepted by the *Telegraaf* for the purpose of glorifying the Dutch deserter. The purest wine has its sediment. It was among such elements that German "agents provocateurs," sent out by the Gestapo, endeavoured to agitate. A small plot which we discovered at Madrigueras was typical in this respect. A systematic attempt was being made to foster dissatisfaction and to organize desertion among some of the war-weary men. The cunningly laid plot never went very far and was unmasked by the soldiers themselves, which proves conclusively how fundamentally sound the men were. Danger lurks not in such provocations, but in the fact that justified grievances are all too easily allowed to remain unrectified. I myself am firmly convinced that a great deal of the so-called war-weariness which finds expression in all manner of small grievances is often due to excessive sexual repression. Nothing is more ridiculous than to represent the combatants in Spain as a band of voluptuaries—a picture drawn, no doubt, by the bourgeois press for the satisfaction of the repressed sexual instincts of its readers. Although the trenches are no bad place for sexual confidences, I cannot remember ever having heard a single story referring to the violation of women and young girls. In fact it is a source of astonishment to me that so little violence was done to women on either side, in spite of Queipo de Llano's obscene incitements. So far as I know only the Moors were guilty and it must be said that they had been lured by the promise of beautiful women.

In their youth journal *La Revolucion*, the Anarchists opened a campaign against masturbation, and from the early days of the war covered the walls of Madrid with posters fervidly calling upon all to fight prostitution, without, however, suggesting an economic basis to ensure its disappearance. At a later stage, the Communists coined the slogan, " every venereal patient is a deserter," an attitude which in my view had grave drawbacks. To prove how depraved the Fascists were, Communist newspapers unanimously cried shame upon the opening of brothels for the different nationalities on the Toledo front.

Needless to say the International Brigades went a step further in this virtuous path. In all the cities and villages where they were garrisoned, the existing brothels were closed. If then venereal diseases broke out among the civilians, as was the case in Madrigueras, supervision became even more severe, and the soldiers were forbidden to visit at their houses. The authorities even went to such lengths as to punish an incautious onanist from barracks No. 4 who had to spend a few days in cell to meditate upon his sins.

In the course of a conversation with the political commissar at the base I was told : " We Communists are against prostitution and a good Communist must be able to control his sexual impulses." Proudly spoken, Mr. Commissar ; but the trouble is that all the soldiers are not Communists, and furthermore you do not take into account the Spanish tradition in such matters, not to mention the primary fact that nature when thwarted takes its revenge.

Another misfortune is the complete non-existence of military handbooks for officers. Whereas a magnificent Spanish history of the world in ten volumes only recently saw the light, the excellent Spanish military regulations have been entirely sold out and are no longer to be obtained for any money. The result is that to the great detriment of uniformity, military drill is arbitrarily carried out in haphazard fashion according to Spanish, German, French, Russian, or Czecho-Slovak methods. The paper shortage is no excuse : the party is continually printing hundreds of thousands of copies of the lives of Stalin, Voroshilov, and Kaganovich, at the same time as innumerable pamphlets on Dnieprostroi and the setting up of crêches. Paper should also be available for printing military regulations.

Another grievance of our militiamen in Madrigueras was that they were totally without Spanish and Catalan newspapers, which gave rise to the circulation of all manner of rumours. I give the explanation of our political commissar for what it is worth : " If we start circulating newspapers here, we cannot according to law prevent the dissemination of the Anarchist press as well, and in proportion to the percentage of Anarchists, who are in the majority."

When I left Madrid on leave for the first time and asked Fermin what I should tell the workers in the West, he answered with a smile : " But that is quite simple, comrade ; tell them the truth and only the truth. It is our best propaganda." A simple man like Fermin had reached the same conclusion as Lassalle, who in his famous allocution, " Proclaim what is," declared this to be the fundamental principle for the whole working class movement. I used to question the truth of this dictum, and for a long time spoke the truth but not the whole truth lest our enemies should use its less favourable aspects to their own advantage. For, as Bergamin once expressed it, it is bitter to think of the satisfaction with which certain utterances are likely to be quoted on the other side of the trench. But I have grown to realize that, while members of the party are silent, the facts speak for themselves, and that we have all the more reason to speak out in proportion as we fear the truth. Our well-meant silence is partly to blame if conditions in Russia have now become so appalling that they can no longer be concealed. In the long run, History is not to be cheated by the wearing of a mask. Even the Allies in the last war have been made to realize that a triumphant war may end in defeat when this victory is based upon a lie. The struggle for socialism cannot be won by the destruction of the enemy if at the same time we destroy socialism within ourselves. The socialist struggle is the struggle for a larger humanity, which can only be attained along the path of truth.

But have we any reason to fear the truth? Certainly not in Spain. The minor critical comments I have made do not in any way tarnish the fair picture as a whole. Except in the Soviet Union, there never was an army such as the Spanish army which was at the same time a living community and a university training centre for a whole nation.

I think of our new libraries in every small village, where of an evening the village lads sit beside our soldiers, playing chess or reading with foreheads puckered in concentration. I think of the thousands of volunteers who celebrated May Day by setting to work on the irrigation canal which at long last was to provide the poor peasants with water. I think of Red Sunday, when whole battalions marched into the vineyards to help the new village collectivization scheme by bringing in the grape harvest. I think of the wounded in Cuevas de la Petita who were saving for a tractor, and of the convalescents in Villanueva de la Jara, who built a gymnastic centre and initiated kindergartens for the village children.

With a feeling of deep tenderness I think of the last children's party we organized in Madrigueras. All the school children had been invited, but we had not reckoned with the likelihood that every boy was going to bring along with him all his younger brothers and sisters, if they were at all able to walk or stand on their feet. The organizing of the procession almost led to a catastrophe ; the little ones stumbled about, began to cry, or lost their shoes, and soon half our soldiers were walking beside the procession carrying children in their arms. Naturally, our supply of gifts was not equal to this added influx of children. In all haste our men went to the village where they bought up the last exercise book, the last pencil, and the last bit of india rubber to be found in the shops. None of the children went home without bearing a gift. The gratitude of the village youth was boundless. When we were marching along the road or exercising in the fields, our soldiers were rigorously forbidden, however great their thirst, to eat of the ripening grapes. Fortunately, we had no right to forbid anything to the village youth and the boys scampered alongside the men, dashing from vine to vine and supplying our soldiers with grapes until their tongues were hanging from their mouths with these exertions.

THE WOUNDED

October 30th, 1937.

THIS IS WHAT I WAS TOLD BY HENK S. WITH WHOM I spent some time in Madrigueras. Suffering from a poisoned cheek, he was lying for some weeks in a hospital solely occupied by patients who had to be artificially fed. The greater part of them had been hit by dum-dum bullets or shell splinters, and had lost their lower jaw with a portion of their vocal organs. Perpetual silence reigned in the wards. Their convalescence was a long martyrdom. Every day the doctors cut from their thighs small pieces of flesh which were then grafted on to the lower part of their cheek. The raw, red flesh gave them a repellent appearance. Many of the foreigners made themselves a nuisance to the nurses owing to their nervous condition. Others, like sick animals, withdrew into themselves, and were filled with sombre forebodings of the future. The Spanish boys, on the other hand, who for the greater part were very young, had apparently learnt from their early youth to suffer hunger, cold, and misery with a certain fatalism. When their conditions improved, they basked in the sun on the terrace or sat on each others' beds playing endless games of lotto. The Head Sister, who was a splendid woman, visited the ward for a quarter of an hour at noon every day, and told them amusing stories. "Then," said Henk, "no sound came from their lips, but from the glint in their eyes you could see that they were laughing inside. When later she went round to each bed, they could only express the depth of their gratitude to her by a helpless, moving gesture of the hand."

After doing all that was possible for their fellow-men, these wounded have now helplessly, but confidently, surrendered themselves to our care. Whatever one may think of their views, it certainly cannot be said that they were actuated by egotistic ambitions. What has humane Europe done for them? We know how from the very beginning the official Red Cross completely neglected its duty towards Government Spain; we know the incredible difficulties that had to be overcome in building up in Spain a proper system of hygiene. In this respect, miracles have been accomplished by well-known doctors, such as Dr. Tegelen, Dr. Walter Blanck, and Dr. Max Hodann, together with an international staff of enthusiastic young helpers. Onteniente was founded by social democracy, and the Scandinavian countries collected thousands of crowns to set up in Alcoy the best hospital in Spain. Nevertheless, the problem of dealing with the growing influx of wounded and sick has remained acute.

Unlike the hospitals in Alcoy and Onteniente, the Dutch hospital in Villanueva de la Jara has been established without financial assistance of any kind from Holland. It owes its birth to the collective idealism of a number of Dutch doctors, nurses, and the political commissar, working in the friendliest cooperation with the Spanish Government. It has a staff of Dutch doctors, superintendents, cooks, chauffeurs, and canteen workers, who within a few weeks gave proof of what can be accomplished by Dutch persistence, Dutch powers of organization, and genuine Dutch comradeship.

Originally the Villanueva hospital was run by an old German doctor, who considered it solely as a sort of physical repair shop for human beings. The building itself—a large castle belonging to a former count—had always stood surly and hostile in the village; this tradition was continued and no contacts existed between the villagers and the patients. In so far as the latter were able to move at all, they went no farther than the nearest café, where they drank more than was good for them and, despite excellent medical attention, acute depression reigned in the wards.

Dr. Voet, however, who had already won his spurs as chief doctor at the Albacete base, had an entirely different conception of his duties. He opened wide the doors to the outside world and the sunlight of a new hope filtered through the stately rooms. " In hospital No. 3 at Albacete," he said to me, " we had a young Dutchman, whose leg, which had been amputated above the knee, continued to swell ; but nothing could break his spirit. Every morning he took up his crutch and went from bed to bed to cheer up the others. It was his daily task, he said. This young man had on his own discovered the surest way to recovery. The necessary will to get well is only to be found in those who do not consider themselves simply as human wrecks, but realize that their lives can continue to be of value to others." I was reminded of a young Spaniard whom I had noticed in hospital a few days ago. He was a fine, well set-up fellow who had lost an arm, and now spent his time in the parlour picking out with one finger the notes of a tune on the piano. Sometimes he would heave a deep sigh as if it were very difficult, but when finally he had reconstructed the little tune, his whole face beamed with a happy smile. Although his thin little tune had begun to bore us all, nobody who had once seen his joy had the courage to say a word. As we had requisitioned the greater number of our nurses from among the peasant girls of the village, Dr. Voet immediately organized a course of lessons to teach them to read and write. A few days later, as I was passing the lesson room, I noticed that this same young man was giving lessons to the girls. His face was even more radiant and more happy than at the piano. He was joking and laughing all the time, and nevertheless seemed an excellent teacher. "And so he is," said Dr. Voet; "and although we are naturally proud of some of the scientific improvements we have introduced—our solarium for tubercular patients, for instance—our main achievement in my view is that we have been successful in making our patients re-establish contacts with life." While I was under treatment at Villanueva, I had every occasion to see that he had not overstated the position. From top to bottom the hospital was a veritable beehive of activity. Painters and designers of advertisements had set up a studio under the roof, where posters, watchwords, and paintings were prepared for the village library, the soldiers' home, and the adornment of the streets. Some four or five boys of the village youth movement attended of an evening and were given drawing lessons. An Austrian carpenter went hobbling about the plaza, where a stand was being built to commemorate the anniversary of the International Brigade. The old church on the hill, partly of

Moorish origin, was being restored and transformed into a club-house. Some vandals had knocked off the head of a very fine Renaissance Madonna and old manuscripts of Gregorian church music lay trampled behind the organ. Everything that could still be retrieved was carried away to a safe place, and a few peasant boys, who helped us with the work, wore a guilty look as they said : " We did not know that such things could have any value." But how could they know ? Who had ever taught the poor to appreciate the value of art ? In this connection a Czech lieutenant hit upon the idea of delivering before the village youth a lecture on Spanish art. They listened with respectful attention ; but, as could be seen from their eyes, the biggest moment of the evening was after the lecture, when a debate took place on the subject of setting up a cultural centre in the church and arrangements were discussed for giving the first mixed dance in the village. It was to be at the same time a musical evening with a choir. The choirmaster was a young German, who told me only the other day that he had but a short time to live. It was found impossible to extract a bullet from under his heart and he was slowly but surely dying of lead poisoning.

And the village children . . . There is no greater friendship than that existing between soldiers and children, or between the children and the wounded. We show them the snapshots we carry about with us. " Look, I too have three little daughters in Holland . . ." And unemotional Piet, who is standing beside me, says in his coarse voice : " See that brat over there . . . that insolent little devil ? The image of my little brother in Holland ! " Perhaps deep down in our hearts we are thinking : " It is for this youth we are struggling. These children will be living when we are dead ; they will continue the struggle for our ideal when we have fallen." But because we do not wish to appear sentimental, we only say out loud : " What damned fine eyes they have in these parts . . ."

The very first night of our arrival, Tim, our energetic Commissar, had summoned a meeting of the delegates of all the wards, with the burgomaster of the village, the teachers, and the committees of the three youth organizations (Left Republican, United Socialist-Communist, and Anarchist Youth Movements). It was agreed after an hour's discussion that conditions in the village school were unworthy of a republican government. Classes of eighty children almost without educational appliances, and housed in an unsuitable old convent—all this had to be changed.

As a first step Dr. Voet suggested a physical examination of all the schoolchildren. With the assistance of Sister Annie a whole day was spent feeling their little ribs and sewing on the buttons of their little trousers. Meanwhile nature-lovers set out on an expedition with the children in order to select a suitable playing field. Another group got busy with distemper and brush and transformed the old stable into a gymnastic centre. A collection among the patients brought in sufficient money to fill a whole ambulance with atlases, books, pencils, and copybooks from Valencia.

This school is the talk of the whole hospital, and well repays a visit. The highest class, with about fifty children—at the time of my visit the remainder were at home helping with the saffron harvest—is held in a low, dark, elongated room with three romanesque windows. Don Alfonso is standing before the class, an aristocratic figure with the pale cheeks of a consumptive. The order maintained in the class is exemplary. Since the master cannot do everything himself, the little ones are helped by some of the bigger boys. As he was taking me round the class to show me their work, it was touching to see the pupils' devotion to him. The little ones were rubbing their heads against him, and some of them playfully seized his hand as he moved on. Excellent work seems to be done, and I am astonished at the subjects with which the children are able to grapple. They were doing history at the time and as I was about to go, Don Alfonso asked me whether I would not like to tell the class something about the history of the Eighty Years War as seen through Dutch eyes. It gave me a curious feeling after so many years to be a teacher once more, and a teacher standing in front of a Spanish class ! But my greatest surprise was when, the lesson being over, I crossed the long, dark passage and entered the old refectory, which was now the classroom of the youngest children. I walked into a blaze of light which was streaming in on all sides. Here, it seemed, measures had been taken without waiting for the help of the International Brigade. The walls were decorated with brightly painted flags and garlands. At the farther end of the room there was a sort of Christmas tree, upon which the little girls were hanging all sorts of objects made by themselves. There were flowers at the windows, aquariums, and a few coloured planks upon which all manner of clay figures were resting which the children themselves were modelling.

" But this is Montessori ! "

" Not exactly," said the fair-haired teacher who met me with a smile ; " we are without the necessary appliances for that. What we have here is a blend of all sorts of systems, which we apply according to our circumstances." I stood rapt in admiration in front of the gaily decorated copybooks : " But this is splendid work ! " The blonde teacher flushed with pleasure : " I am delighted to hear you say that. The Commandant of the aerodrome recently paid us a visit with his adjutant, and he too was pleased with what he saw. I suspect, however, that you know a little more about teaching."

" I was a teacher myself."

" I thought so by the way you picked up those copybooks." Naturally, I was then called upon to admire little Domingo, the mathematical genius, and Pepita, who recites so well, and José's drawings, which are to be sent to the exhibition for school-children's work in Barcelona. It was not necessary to be an expert to see that the results obtained were far above the average. " But how do you manage it," I asked, " with so many children ? "

She pointed to two plainly dressed women who were moving from one little table to the other, helping the children. " They are two village girls whom I have trained myself and whom I pay from my own salary." And then she added hastily : " But that is no sacrifice. The school is all I have in the world. Early in life when I wanted to become a teacher, my parents were against it. It was not considered proper for a girl of my class to work. I went through with it, however. I left my home, and by so doing, broke with all my relations and acquaintances. Immediately after my examination I came here, and my only wish in the world is to remain. Why should children in another town be more likeable than these? The parents have confidence in me, and when on Sundays I go to the mountains, I am always accompanied by some ten or fifteen of my pupils."

Returning to hospital I began talking about the school to a young Catalan militiaman with whom I had struck up a friendship. He interrupted me by saying, "I have no brothers any more." I asked him what he meant.

"I was in Barcelona when the town was bombarded. Of course they had heard from their spies that all our chasers were on the Aragon front. They refrained from flying over the centre of the town because it was defended by anti-aircraft guns. Instead, they flew over our district; first their heavy bombers and then the chasers. The tri-motors dropped bombs of five hundred kilos, and six story buildings collapsed like houses of cards. Everybody rushed out into the street in panic—and you know how broad and straight the streets are in Barcelona. Then the chasers followed and flying very low machine-gunned the population during the stampede. For almost half an hour I lay on my belly in the gutter because the 'planes returned again and again. Suddenly the rumour went round that they were busy bombing the San Pablo school.

Immediately forgetting all danger, I sprang up, for my little brothers were in that school. There could be no possible doubt : they were flying low round and round the building and encircling it. Before I was able to get there, they had registered a direct hit. That morning, two hundred children in this school were killed or wounded. My little brothers were among them, but we were only able to recover two of the three bodies . . ."

I was unexpectedly recalled to Albacete, where I was informed that I had been given leave for a tour of propaganda. At the same time, from headquarters an order came through that I was to escort a group of thirty disabled soldiers to Paris.

I found them waiting for me in the local hostel—at first sight a pitiful group of human wrecks. Two of them had lost both legs ; a number of them one arm ; others were minus an eye and a few, their bodies twitching all over, were suffering from shell-shock. All were feeling nervous and cold in the uncomfortable posada, as they were waiting impatiently for the train which was due at midnight and was more than four hours late. When finally it steamed into the station we found that the carriage reserved for us had somehow filled up on the way with women and children evacuated from Madrid. I noted their emaciated, exhausted faces, the sleeping children, and the miserable luggage. Nevertheless, there seemed to be no alternative but to relegate them to the goods-truck at the end of the train, which was still fairly empty. It was then that my new charges revealed themselves to me and that I was made to realize the stuff of which they were made. While I was still negotiating with the stationmaster, they were having an earnest conversation among themselves and then a young Czech stepped out and walked straight up to me: "Captain," he said "the legless must get in here, but so far as we are concerned, there is room enough in the goods-truck. Let the women stay where they are." When I sprang into the truck, having at long last collected a few bundles of straw, just as the train was about to move, I found that they had already settled themselves down among the luggage and were singing tunes from the international song book, while one of them was lighting up the pages with an electric torch.

My first impression of these people, who were physically, but not spiritually, broken was confirmed in the course of the next days I was to spend with them—days which were difficult and dreadful in the extreme.

The trouble began in Valencia, where we had expected to catch the direct connection for Barcelona. Just when our great offensive at Fuentes del

Ebro had begun and our advance posts had already occupied the Northern station in Saragossa, nature crossed our plans. A fearful rainstorm broke out. In a few hours the rivers were swollen ; bridges and whole villages were washed away and the harvest, the cattle, the roads, and the railway were destroyed in the Ebro valley. Just when the seat of the Government was being removed, direct connection between Barcelona and Valencia was interrupted for weeks. For a time there was danger that the foe would take advantage of this state of things to order an attack upon our coast from Majorca. At the front the offensive was brought to a standstill ; the reserves could not be brought up ; guns and munitions remained sticking in the mud, and in a few hours entire trench systems were washed away as if they had never been.

And so we were left for hours in the waiting-room of the station in Valencia, where no bed was to be had, because a ship with more than 6,000 refugees had arrived that very morning from Gijon.

All day long we waited, but not until nightfall was I able to obtain accommodation for us in a hospital a long way out of town, where, I hasten to add, the very greatest care and friendly attention was bestowed upon us. There we were cooped up for forty-eight hours while our boys, who were longing to get back home, were growing more and more nervous and excited. But still the permanent way continued to be several feet under water at various points. There was no alternative but to obtain two large French lorries and do the journey by the long roundabout road through Aragon.

But our troubles had only begun. As fate would have it, the motor of our second lorry went wrong as we were crossing the first mountain-pass. For the remainder of the journey we had to drag it along with us, and the men in the first lorry had to sit shut up without light and with no view, while the two lorries shivered and jerked along the deep ravines, where time and again we found the road blocked for hours by all manner of transport.

Upon arriving at night in a village suspended in the unearthly quiet of the mountainside, I had to alight and seek my way through the darkened streets, looking for beds for my comrades, who were waiting and shivering in the lorries. One of them, who had been shot in the stomach, required hot milk ; but there was no milk to be had anywhere. Wounds had to be examined, cleaned, and dressed, but the orderly, whom I had with me, had not counted upon so long a journey and was short of dressings. In the mornings and again at midday, I had to enter into arduous food negotiations with the burgomaster of the villages through which we passed. Thousands of soldiers had already trekked through these usually deserted regions, and as a rule nothing more was to be got from the peasants whether for love or money. Of the two I found love to be the more potent agency. When I had pleaded long enough on behalf of my wounded, I was almost invariably successful in the end in getting a few eggs or a rabbit that had been put by for domestic requirements, although I confess I had to break the law at times and pay more than the official maximum price. But what was the poor pelican to do when he knew that his young were waiting with wide-open bills? An even more tragic moment was when the wounds of the young Czech, which appeared to have healed up entirely after seven months in hospital, began to give further trouble.

It took us more than four days to cover those 400 miserable kilometres to Barcelona. When finally we crossed the frontier at Cerbère, I said to Jan, the Fleming, who had lost both his legs, "Well, for you the struggle is over." He gave me a reproachful look.

"No, Comrade," he said, "the struggle goes on."

VALE

November 7th, 1937.

THE ATMOSPHERE OF THE HÔTEL MAJESTIC IN THE Paseo de Gracia had all the decorum of a first-class hotel in the heart of London. Noiselessly both waiters and guests went about on their lawful occasions. Ministers and Consuls were clutching their glimmering attaché cases in which they seemed to be carrying the salvation of the world. Ladies " en grand décolleté " were performing complicated ceremonies with lipstick and powder. In the hall, where the telephone boxes were not for a moment unoccupied, a small army of journalists had pitched their tents ; they were perpetually in conversation with various important personalities, from whom they were seeking information as to the exact course of events in the interior. My worn-out field attire looked shabby beside all these gilded uniforms of generals, and the lounge suit, for which I had been measured that morning, would not be ready for twenty-four hours.

With Captain Smircka, still the most active officer

on the staff of the International Brigade, though eleven times wounded, I went out into the town. He wanted to get a few luxury articles to take back to his wife and, certainly, he could not have complained that his choice was limited. I was astounded by the sumptuousness and good taste of the display in the large establishments. I can strongly recommend a shopping expedition to Barcelona to any lady who wishes to dress smartly. She will discover that in the matter of fashion and taste, Barcelona is not to be outdone by Paris.

A double decker took us to the gay Rambla. All the cafés were packed with people, and in the restaurants we discovered that a very good meal was still to be had for twenty or thirty pesetas. A bootblack refused my tip. But how stupid of me! I should have remembered that the bootblacks are organized here, and that they only work on a fixed tariff.

Yes, for twenty or thirty pesetas, there is still very decent food to be got in Barcelona, but bread, the staple food of the Spanish people, is not to be had, and a casual labourer is not likely to earn much more than ten pesetas a day. Where the sewers discharge into the sea, I saw boys of twelve and fourteen standing with bare feet in the cold water: they had been fishing all day for scrap metal in the mud. According to what they themselves affirmed, they could make two pesetas a day if they had any luck.

With blissful memories of the Valencia seafront, I asked the way to the Playa. Between endless factories and sheds I reached a rickety stair that led to a narrow strip of sand. On this narrow strip, between seawall and sea, were hovels . . .

In Madrid I came to know all about the working-class dwellings of the suburbs ; the mud floor, the absence of windows, drains, and chimneys. In Cuenca I had seen the cave dwellings of the poor hacked out of the wall of the mountains. In Valencia, opposite the hospital where we had been put up, I had derived a very peculiar architectonic impression of Spanish poverty. What I saw was an apparently flat surface upon which merely chimneys were erected. Upon closer inspection I was able to discern, between these chimneys, deep holes sloping downwards and leading to the entrance of a dwelling. Here and there, there was also some wire-netting stretched across a rectangular hole : a court-yard. Human beings had buried themselves here in the rocky soil, like moles or rabbits. Reckoned out in wages, each of these houses would have cost a fortune, but they who built them did not require to pay wages. One does not require to pay wages to oneself. They had only to consider the economy in building material, the rocky soil serving at the same time as wall and roof. Since they had no doctor when they became ill, doctors' bills for rheumatism and tuberculosis never constituted a part of their budget.

But these subterranean holes, or even the caravans of gipsies, struck me as veritable palaces compared with the hovels on the Barcelona water-front, threatened by every storm at sea. The rotting boards were washed by the waves ; the roofs consisted of flattened-out tins ; the window-panes, of glass fragments eked out with paper where necessary. As I saw them that afternoon the inhabitants of these hovels could certainly be described as subhuman. Clad in rags, dirty, neglected, and unkempt, they were lounging and sitting on their doorsteps. For all my curiosity, it was some long time before I ventured down into the little street. They looked me up and down as if I had been a hostile foreigner. There was nobody here to raise the clenched fist and to say "*salud.*"

Upon reaching the end of the alley, I turned to retrace my steps, only to find that my retreat had been cut off. A brawl had suddenly flared up in the middle of the street, and the air resounded with bestial cries and curses. Two young fellows in their torn shirts were going for each other, and every moment I expected knives to flash out. A boy of twelve was dancing round the other two, shrieking like a wild dervish and hurling stones at his brother's assailant. A few women came rushing up to me in tears : " *Ay, madre mia*, do separate them, Captain ; there will be murder in a moment." It suddenly came to me that I had left my revolver at home ; I found myself in the unpleasant position of a policeman without a weapon. I felt I was running the risk of being set upon by the whole street if I went meddling with their business. How I managed it, I don't know, but to make a lòng story short I found myself at a certain moment between the two combatants, who were being held down by the women, and saying something to the effect that we really had something better to do at such a time as this than to be flying at each others' throats. With shrugs and curses the aggressor withdrew, but the little brother had to be forcibly disarmed, for he was already preparing to go after him with a stone. The other boy, whom I was now holding down, had broken down completely. He was crying with rage and calling upon heaven and hell to witness that he was no deserter : " I'm no deserter, Captain, that's a lie of that scallywag's ; I can show you my papers ; I was rejected because of my bad lungs."

On my way back to the Hôtel Majestic I had ample time to consider the difference between the Russian civil war and the Spanish. The hirelings of the reactionary press are quite wrong in their maunderings over red Spain. There is no need for such anxious forebodings ; their capitalist " order," with the necessary differences between rich and poor, continues in Barcelona as before. The Spanish people are not yet defending the results of a social revolution, but only their hope for a better future, including that of sub-humans who wish to become human beings.

Our train was stationed so long at Port Bou that it looked as if it were part of our programme to wait for the daily arrival of the Fascist bombers. In the waiting-room the entire furniture, including all the bottles of the former buffet, had been smashed to smithereens by a bomb. But Lissone's posters were still hanging quite undamaged on the wall.

" Go to Spain and have a different holiday ! "

" Spain . . . the romance of the East and the comfort of the West ! "

And underneath, in German :

" Visit Spain . . . ; a thousand wonders await thee ! "

I smiled ; these wonders were made manifest to the German hirelings at Guadalajara, Brunete, Belchite, and Quinto !

Right across the platform a red piece of canvas was still suspended, which now had begun to fade.

It was in French: "Free men from all over the world, the free peoples of Iberia welcome you. Catalonia and Spain salute you!"

And, verily, free men from all over the world came to Spain to help the Spanish people in the struggle for their freedom and their future. This, too, is a wonder only to be seen in Spain and one not easily to be forgotten.

RETROSPECT

Stockholm, January 1938.

FROM ALL SIDES I WAS ADVISED NOT TO PUBLISH MY "letters from Spain," as they were written and as they here appear. A kind friend wrote from Holland:

"From every quarter he will be attacked and persecuted. His best comrades will isolate him if they can. If they do not murder him with weapons, they will attempt to starve him into submission. They will spread rumours about him and tell his comrades at the front that he fled from them like a coward. Against their better judgment he will be dubbed a Trotskyist, only to be reviled and persecuted by the Trotskyists. The *Volk* newspaper will be furtively jubilant at his conversion, and the *Volksdagblad* will bellow something about "corrupt intellectuals" à la Gide and Last. Boris Raptschinsky will write a smart and mannered article in the *Handelsblad* about the revulsion of feeling that has come over "the best spirits in Red Spain" who have been taught by grim experience what "brutish humanity" is like, but who, like all revolutionary socialists, are too unintelligent to realize yet that society is changing. The *Telegraaf* will issue a warning that one of the leaders of the press-gang has returned to Holland to lure a few more innocent victims to the ' perilous land of murder.' In short, anybody who arrives at a definite and personal point of view is outlawed, because freedom of opinion in general is frowned upon and, consequently, outlawed."

I have good reason to believe that this is only a tame description of what awaits me as a stateless writer without legal rights. Nevertheless, I do not see why the prospect should restrain me since I already settled my account with life in the trenches, and can only now consider what remains of it as an undeserved extra. In any case I should consider it an act of betrayal to myself not to communicate to others my spiritual experience.

I should be more tempted to keep silence on other grounds which were forcibly brought home to me a few days ago when two German refugees came to visit me here in Stockholm, immediately after I had addressed the Clarté group on the subject of " Don Quixote in the Trenches." One of them told me that his brother, who had worked for the Party for fifteen years, had been expelled from the Soviet Union at the same time as hundreds of other Germans, in spite of the article in the constitution guaranteeing the right of asylum. His expulsion was not on grounds of opposition but only because he did not wish to assume Russian citizenship. Since then he had roamed through Europe as a refugee, which means that he was denied work, and the means of living or of founding a legal home anywhere. He now had drifted to Paris with a view to enrolling as a volunteer for Spain. Although he had never taken action against the Party, the suspicions aroused by his expulsion from the Soviet Union were so great that he had already been kept waiting six months without means of subsistence. His brother had come to ask me if I could do anything to enable him to recover the right to fight for his ideals and, if necessary, to die for them.

That opposition should be punished with a prohibition to continue the struggle ; that one is cut off from the masses ; that perhaps it will never be possible for me to lead my company in the last settling of accounts with Franco—this is the bitterest thought of all. But I must learn to face this, too. Indeed, whoever refuses to speak after the Moscow trials deserves for his betrayal and craven-heartedness the eternal contempt of the masses.

If I have to justify myself, it is not for speaking out now, but for having been silent so long.

For years it has been customary in Holland to

consider me as a purblind, fanatical partisan of Stalinism. This view is so prevalent as to make people overlook the unmistakably critical comments in many of my articles, and in my book *Een Huis zonder Vensters.* As a matter of fact, I went over to Communism not straight from the Social Democratic Party, but through the Schmidt Movement and the Anarchist-Trotskyist School of Sneevliet. I had read practically everything that had been written by the opposition, and on my very first visit to Russia, in 1930, was made to realize that much of their criticism was justified. Already then, at the back of the Trade Union Palace, excited and desperate workers showed me their worn-out shoes and the hovels in which they lived, saying : " Do the workers in Europe live like this ? " Already then, I had conversations with students who revealed to me an entirely different side of life from that which is usually shown to tourists.

In 1932 I lived nine months in Moscow in a ramshackle place in which nobody would dare accommodate the poorest Dutch family. I saw at close range the boundless corruption that was prevalent among the leading Russian writers ; I became personally acquainted with such figures as Serge and Kliuiev, and knew to what persecutions they were exposed. I had contacts with Russian peasants who lived in cellars, compared with which Gorki's

Dosshouse was paradise. Later, in 1936, my journey to Russia with André Gide brought me to the verge of despair. Alas ! I knew Russian too well, and had too many connections among all sections of the population, to allow myself to be deceived by outward appearance.

Is my honesty to be impugned because I refrained from publication ?

Entirely of my own free will, and without expecting or obtaining any advantages, I had become a member of the Dutch Communist Party. In the Sneevliet group I had found the same barren negations which had always prevented Trotsky from exercising an influence upon the masses. I had come to realize that no mass movement can be built up on mere criticism which is allied to opportunist action. I realized that to discredit the revolution itself by denying its results and by depriving the working classes of future hope was to throw away the child with the bath water. I had a great personal respect for the genius and integrity of Trotsky, but his system diverged only tactically from that of Stalin. It sprang from the same juristic-rabbinical root ; its methods were morally as ruthless, and in my view, it would not have worked very differently from Stalinism, had it been put to the test of practice.

Weapons are required to wage the class war. The Parties must needs be accounted a portion of our armament. When we set out from Madrid for the Sierra, we defended ourselves with shot-guns. Our realization of their inadequacy in a war against a modern army did not induce us to throw away the only firearms we possessed. We wage war for socialism, not because proletarians are angels, but because capitalism has adulterated and corrupted whatever was originally good in men. The Parties created by man for the purpose of furthering the struggle are as imperfect as man himself. You stick to your shot-gun so long as no better firearm is available, and so long as you have one shot left. At the same time, whoever joins in the game must adhere to the rules of the game, and whoever is member of a party must submit to its discipline. No word or act of mine was directed against the party until I left the party as a result of the Moscow trials, and of Russia's inadequate support of the Spanish Republic which became manifest at the fall of Teruel.

Whoever has learnt to think dialectically knows that there is no such thing as "either, or," that shadow is one of the conditions for the existence of light, and that the two sides of a coin cannot lie in the sun at the same time. Only naïve souls hanker after a heaven without shadow, and even so they have to conjure up hell as a contrast, in order properly to enjoy their blessed state. The Russian revolution is and was neither the perfect paradise depicted by some of its champions nor the hell depicted by the capitalists. It always was and had to be a dialectical unity of opposites. The revolution should be judged not by taking a cross section at any given moment, but by considering the resultant forces, the synthesis towards which the whole movement is trying to evolve. So long as any hope was left that in this process the revolutionary forces would triumph over the counter-revolutionary, it might well have seemed a crime to further these counter-revolutionary forces by criticism which could be taken advantage of by the enemy against the revolution itself. In the life and death struggle which the working classes are now waging against Fascism, it might have seemed misguided and gratuitous to alienate the only potentially powerful ally at our disposal.

In the face of all Bourgeois and Anarchistic criticism, it must be stated that the Russian revolution, far from being a failure, was a tremendous historical stepping-stone on the road to socialism, the importance of which it would be impossible to overestimate.

The liberation of mankind demands as a prerequisite condition a planned control of the forces of production, which in a capitalist society are chaotic and therefore oppressive to mankind. To the Soviet Union belongs the imperishable honour of having carried out the first five year plan ever launched, and all the subsequent plans of Roosevelt, of Social Democracy, and of Hitler only confirm the prestige attached to this first plan. For the first time in history a State was able to overcome the fatal iron cycle of crisis following upon crisis. Only those who have felt in their bones the deteriorating effects of unemployment, not only on the physical but also and more particularly on the moral plane, can fully grasp the superiority of socialist methods of production which have made an end to unemployment.

The Soviet Union proved for the first time in the history of mankind that a whole people can live without the mysticism of the Church. At a time when Kollontai wrote *Free Love*, it proved also that a very considerable degree of sexual freedom constitutes no danger to society as a whole. At a time when Jews and Negroes are once more being sent out like scapegoats into the wilderness, and the insanity of the race theory is rampant in the world, the Soviet Union has carried out a racial and national policy which, whatever its defects, can certainly serve as an example to every other country. Not only was illiteracy abolished, but the Soviet

Union contrived to awaken throughout the masses a profound and live interest in the arts and sciences such as is to be found nowhere else. The significance of this achievement is not by any means lessened by the deplorable and unprogressive examples of bad taste with which this hunger is being more and more satisfied.

The Soviet Union has no imperialistic aspirations. It never strove to recover the regions it had lost, and as a result of its peace policy, it preserved us for years from a new world war.

Its agricultural policy, with all the successes and setbacks of collectivization, is the most heroic experiment in history and an object lesson for the future. The emancipation of women, even after the prohibition of abortion and the many reactionary measures which more recently have again reduced the status of women, constitutes an enormous step forward. One could fill libraries with the records of what has been accomplished in the spheres of hygiene and child welfare. Naturally the development of industry at a more than American tempo, and the building up of a powerful army, do not in themselves constitute socialism, but these achievements certainly do constitute the necessary foundations for its development and defence. What is even more important, they testify to the fact that the bourgeoisie are no particularly intelligent and indispensable species of human beings, and that they can be replaced within a few years by forces springing exclusively from the masses of the people. The theory that some are born to lead and others born to serve was destroyed in Russia by the practice of the revolution. In those days, Lenin, Trotsky, and Stalin were merely the instruments for carrying out the will of the masses. They were carried forward by these masses because they consciously set out to interpret and carry out the latter's wishes. When the country was invaded on fourteen fronts by the armies of Wrangel and Koltchak, the invaders were driven out, not by a dictator, but by the people themselves. With boundless self-sacrifice the misery of famine was overcome and the foundations of reconstruction laid not by any dictator but by the people themselves and their councils.

The Russian revolution is a triumphant proof of the power of the masses to create cultural values. Its stream only began to silt up when criticism, one of the greatest creative forces of the people, was suppressed. A soulless discipline was introduced, destructive of all criticism—except, needless to say, such criticism as was directed against the opposition—and, with every window closed, the air became so fetid as to make it impossible for any healthy person to remain any longer inside the Third International.

And yet, viewed historically, even the introduction of this soulless discipline was to be understood. The Third International had before its eyes an example of a party completely bereft of discipline, that of the Second International, where congress decisions were taken only to be forgotten as soon as possible, where the word, International, was only a pretext for international congresses with impressive resolutions, but where in practice every country merely pursued the path prescribed by its own narrow interest. Owing to lack of discipline and international solidarity, the Second International became a negligible factor in international policy from 1914 onwards.

We have been repeatedly intimidated by the assurance that every criticism of the Soviet Union and the Third International was criminal, because it would be used by the reaction and by Fascism as a weapon against the proletariat. This assertion has proved unwarranted. The Soviet Union's loss of credit with the masses is due to its own deeds and not to our criticism. One single trial at Moscow has had a more potent effect than could be achieved by a hundred books of Gide. Furthermore, it is no longer enough to be silent ; whoever wishes to defend the recent policy of the Soviet Union is compelled more and more to resort deliberately to pretence and prevarication.

But so great are the elements of truth still residing in the movement that we must guard against allowing our criticism to breed a spirit of indifference among the masses. Nor must we slur over the faults committed by the other parties, whose responsibility for the final catastrophe has been at least as great as that of the Communists, and whose responsibility for the course of events in Russia is also not to be denied.

We were taught in the trenches to look upon cowardice as the gravest sin of all. It looks more and more as if the entire youth of Europe were now of the same opinion. Cowardice was the original sin of the Second International. From cowardice it permitted towards the end of its days the murders of Karl Liebknecht and Rosa Luxemburg. Cowardice and the spirit of President Ebert, who "hated the revolution like sin," gave us the bloodhound, who was the undoing of the workers of the Ruhr; through cowardice the downfall of the Hungarian and Bavarian Soviet Republics was consummated, and cowardice presided over the constitution of every coalition with the bourgeois parties. Cowardice permitted Zörgiebel to shoot down the workers of Wedding on May Day; it voted for Hindenburg and armoured cruisers, and prevented the general strike when Hitler came into power. It induced the party members of the

Reichstag to vote for Hitler's foreign policy to the tune of Germany's national anthem and the trade union leaders to order the party members to celebrate May Day together with the Nazis. Cowardice is the only truly international characteristic of the Second International, and was responsible in the end for Blum's initiative in the matter of non-intervention, which has cost the lives of hundreds of thousands of the flower of Spanish youth.

It would be worse than foolish, however, to pretend that leaders or members were guilty of personal cowardice : this wanton accusation could only further hinder the reconciliation of the various wings of the working class movement. Nothing has been so conducive to the rise of Fascism as these reciprocal cries of betrayal which have destroyed confidence within the movement itself. The overwhelming majority of these people were moved by honest conviction and many of them subsequently gave proof of their unshakeable personal courage and conviction in the law courts, the concentration camp, or, like Julius Deutsch, in Spain. The cowardice of which we speak springs from a mistaken theory, according to which it must always be assumed that only direct material interests need be taken into account, and not the magnificent reserves of sacrifice and idealism that lie hidden in the people. Often, too, it has been the outcome of an exaggerated sense of responsibility which quailed at the very thought of acts of violence to which the opposing party was prepared to resort with an easy conscience.

Undoubtedly Trotsky was right when he affirmed that socialism could not be built up in one country alone ; it was equally clear, however, that on the basis of this pessimistic proclamation there was nothing to be done in Russia as soon as the proletariat of western Europe proved to be hopelessly unequal to the situation. Revolution happens not to be an article for export, and it became necessary to endeavour to make the best of things in isolation and surrounded by foes. Distrust of the revolutionary will of the proletariat drove Russia to an alliance with the capitalist States which naturally was only to be purchased at the expense of extensive capitulations and concessions. By 1935, I was able to observe in national Mohammedan circles in Morocco the extent to which the attitude of the Soviet Union was driving the disappointed nationalists of the colonial countries towards the Right. No further trust was placed in a State which denounced Italian aggression in Geneva, and at the same time multiplied its friendly offices to Italy, to which it calmly went on delivering grain and oil. And worse was to follow : Italian aeroplanes over Madrid were fed with Russian oil.

In 1933 the Soviet Union disillusioned the whole world proletariat, when its only reply to Hitler's *coup d'état* was to extend its commercial agreement with Germany. Its greatest error, however, was committed in 1936 when, in contrast to Mexico, it signed the non-intervention agreement for the sake of a doubtful alliance with France ; by faithfully adhering to the agreement until October 23rd, the Soviet Union deprived the Spanish Republic of the arms with which in the beginning it could easily have triumphed.

The constant menace of war made it necessary for the Soviet Union to build up its industry on an unbalanced basis, first place being given to armament production. It was compelled to strengthen its centralized bureaucracy and to resort to non-socialist methods to force up production. The danger of an inadequate food supply necessitated the granting of more and more concessions to the peasants. All these concessions have resulted in the emergence of a new privileged class which now is ruthlessly and consistently using the power of the State to defend its own interests and future.

Marxism defines the State as an institution based upon power and violence and controlled by a ruling class for the purpose of repressing the other classes. Marxism aims at the gradual elimination of the

State and its substitution by a classless society, in which repression will cease to have any purpose. The means to attain this end is the dictatorship of the proletariat. No real dictatorship is, however, intended ; the only object of this dictatorship being that those who live not by work, but by exploitation, and who therefore are interested in the perpetuation of the exploitation of man by man, shall be deprived of their political rights. The dictatorship of the proletariat is democratic in the sense that it is a centralized democracy ; in other words, all decisions are debated and taken at the base. The executive merely carries out these decisions while all sections are compelled to submit to these decisions once they have been laid down.

Leninism rejects bourgeois democracy and parliamentarism as being only sham democracy, in which the really important organized units are withdrawn from the influence of the people. (At Eindhoven, for instance, Philips has more to say than the town council ; even in the case of mines owned by the State, power is in the hands of a bureaucracy which is entirely alien to the men who work the mines.) Leninism aims at a condition of things where " every kitchenmaid will be able to control the State " ; in other words, where every individual consciously bears responsibility for the general weal. The road towards the gradual elimination of the State leads through the Soviets, i.e. through self-government by the federally built-up organized units. In the factory Soviet, in the Soviet of house dwellers, or in that of the parents of school-going children, temporary representatives, who are known and trusted, are elected and these organizations, built up in the shape of a pyramid and interconnected, draw up legislation for themselves in their own sphere and organize the authority with which the laws are maintained and carried out. The geographical boundaries of these Soviets do not coincide with those of the States. A cultural Soviet pyramid can be based on uniformity of language, while an electricity Soviet is based upon a particular generating station and its radiation. Every active citizen is connected with a number of Soviets and only the unproductive individual is excluded from political influence. Since the community is organized on the basis of trades and occupations and not upon ideologies, businesslike discussions, restricted to the field where debate is fruitful, take the place of vague political discussions. This is the essential factor which differentiates the Soviet system from Fascism as well as from Bourgeois Democracy : the masses are not governed by representation, they govern themselves. They do not require a father or a redeemer to clear up their little affairs for them while they remain under tutelage. The masses govern themselves, and by shouldering responsibility are able to ripen to maturity.

Thus is the State gradually eliminated according to the Marxist conception. But what do we see in Russia? The State in Russia is stronger than ever. If, therefore, the Marxist definition be correct, we are compelled to ask ourselves against which class its power is directed, and which new class is being protected. Indeed, nobody is likely to believe that *all* the old collaborators of Lenin and *all* the great figures from the revolutionary period belong to the capitalist class that has disappeared.

All the signs are pointing in the same direction. One of the most typical characteristics of the new Russia is the propaganda which is again being conducted in favour of the family and parental authority. If now we refer to Friedrich Engels's *Origin of the Family, Private Property and the State*, we shall see that the family is no primeval institution, but an institution evolved out of the patriarchal system for the protection of property and inheritance and which has served as the foundation for the entire subsequent development of capitalist society. In Russia, matters have now reached a stage where congresses are held of "the wives of Red officers," or "the wives of industrial leaders," in which, therefore, women are considered as acting no longer in their own right but merely in their capacity of domestic companion and appendage to man. Furthermore, divorce has already been made considerably more difficult and the law prohibiting abortion deprives women of the right to dispose of their own person. Finally, the Soviet Constitution now guarantees the right of inheritance.

It has been asserted that this right of inheritance applies only to the means of consumption, and not to the means of production, which alone would constitute the real touchstone. This, however, is incorrect. Deposits are constantly increasing in the Soviet savings banks, and these banks pay seven per cent. interest. According to every Marxist definition, this interest is unearned income, i.e. surplus value, which goes not to the producers of this surplus value but to others ; in other words it is a form of exploitation. Just as the shareholder in capitalist countries is joint owner in a company's means of production, so the Russian citizen who has put his money in a State bank is joint owner of the means of production of the State. An Alexei Tolstoi earns a million roubles a year ; one should bear in mind what this yearly sum with accumulated interest is likely to represent for his heirs as unearned income.

Since the decline of the factory councils, the management of State production as well as the distribution of its profits is in the hands of a class of bureaucrats, technocrats, and " engineers of the soul " (artists) ; they now have no contacts with the actual workers except at meetings, and in their everyday lives they keep them at a distance in the most lower middle-class fashion. Their wives subscribe to the new fashionable journals, wear dressing-gowns, cover themselves in scent and powder, and use lipstick, while they themselves are the men who in the new Moscow frequent the bars and night resorts that are springing up like toadstools everywhere. Their servants buy up the expensive luxuries in " Gastronom " and the other stores which are the delight of workers' delegations. These are the people who together with the privileged members of the closed party put up at the hotels and model rest houses—which are extremely scarce in proportion to the total population—on the Russian riviera. At the really excellent hotel where we stayed in Sukhum-Kaleh, a room cost a thousand roubles a month, but the chambermaid, who was not allowed to eat in the kitchen of the hotel, earned ninety roubles a month. With a family of five she lived behind the establishment in a gruesome hovel without water or lavatory accommodation, or any of the usual conveniences, in a room measuring two and a half metres by three. Her eldest boy, an asthma patient, was crowded out and slept on the doorstep at nights rolled up in a blanket. Since warm food in the Stolovaia cost one rouble sixty-five, the family could only permit itself this luxury once or twice in the week.

In Sochi where there was dancing every night and where drunken guests were in the habit of throwing the table silver into the sea, the smallest packet of cigarettes in our hotel cost eight roubles, but the workmen, who were asphalting the road in front of the hotel, dressed only in shorts, earned five roubles a day. At Sevastopol we were again entertained by the writers to an endless supper with roast sucking pig and a whole procession of bottles of vodka, wines, and liqueurs. When finally at eleven o'clock at night we got up and left almost in a state of congestion, we noticed that tramps were lying asleep on newspapers in the street. In Sevastopol alone Herbart and I spoke to twenty-seven of them. Ten of them were living under a porch by the harbour just beside the new Dynamo stadium, where the youthful élite of the town went to bathe and cnjoy themselves. A woman doctor informed us that several of these tramps had had to be shot owing to repeated robbery and murder. Political agents assured us that there was no room left in the institutions for children, "because in the Winter all the riff-raff come to the Crimea and remain hanging about for the rest of the time." Whoever studies Soviet statistics will note a very considerable rise in the total expenditure for wages. This total sum includes the salaries of the most highly paid technicians and even of the most highly placed officials. Yet the wages of the most numerous group, that of the unskilled labourers, remain unaltered at from ninety to a hundred and twenty roubles a month. The rise in production has therefore benefited to an ever-increasing degree a few privileged groups. It may well be asked how one is to live on a wage of ninety roubles a month, when a kilogram of butter of second best quality costs fifteen roubles, an inferior suit of clothes two hundred roubles, a pair of shoes between thirty and sixty roubles, a ticket on the underground one rouble, and so on and so forth. It should also be borne in mind that the Stakhanov system is already in itself an exploitation and separates the proletariat into two classes with conflicting interests. Whereas the shock-worker on the basis of the piece wage system was paid more in proportion to his increased output, the Stakhanov system is based upon a premium over and above the piece wage when a certain limit has been exceeded. Anybody who is at all conversant with the various wage systems will recognize here Gausch's differential wage and American sweating. It is not difficult to see that any system involving a premium implies a payment above the achievement which can only be met out of the general wage fund, and which therefore can only be effected at the expense of the other workers. While it is true that increased production may result in a rise in the general level of existence—as is the case in all capitalist countries—this increase, coupled with increased differentiation and exploitation, is always theoretical and is felt by the masses as tending towards relative pauperization.

Undoubtedly the workers' delegations from the West can be shown contented workers who live in a three-roomed dwelling, and, to judge from certain photographs, these dwellings usually contain even a piano. It remains a mystery, however, how this improvement can be brought about in a city like Moscow, where the number of inhabitants outpaces building operations in the ratio of four to one, while at the same time a number of relatively new houses have already become practically uninhabitable. But the clue is to be found in the new law, which permits families to be ejected from their homes even when no alternative can be offered them, provided that compensation be granted at the rate of five hundred roubles a head. And so, many families of the lowest groups have had to make way to provide more living accommodation for the Stakhanov workers or more space for the frenzied building of palaces with which it is hoped to outvie Chancellor Hitler. In view of the fact that a flat in the co-operative new building of the writers costs nine thousand roubles, one can imagine what the hovels must look like which the ejected workers usually build for themselves from waste wood on the fringe of Moscow. Needless to say that the assertion that every worker in the Soviet Union can become a Stakhanovist is just as foolish as the assertion that every newspaper boy in America can become a millionaire. Nevertheless, it awakens the same illusions. But this illusion that one individual is capable of rising above the masses was precisely the greatest obstacle on the road to socialism during the years of American prosperity. To honour as a socialist hero somebody who in reality is only a pronounced type of go-getter or who, while entirely lacking in idealism and general culture, happens to have a particular knack for a thing and does it to perfection, must lead to boundless mental confusion. These Stakhanov workers, together with the bureaucracy, the technocracy, and the " engineers of the soul " live better and are better housed than the masses thanks to their disproportionate salaries. They spend their time in small coteries and circles, and hate modern " degenerate " art with that lower middle class hatred which is so prevalent in Germany. It is not surprising that the artistic exhibits in the Russian and German pavilions in the Paris Exhibition were so strikingly alike, and that the new moral code of the Soviet Union can be subscribed to by any pastor in Staphorst. The toadying portrait painters of Stalin are paid out of all proportion to their deserts, but Surrealists, Constructivists, or simply Modernists are not to be found west of Siberia. At Tiflis we were permitted to visit an exhibition where every painting represented a period of Stalin's life. These canvases were about as worthless as the decorations at a country fair. Of the critique sent in by Masereel, who was with us at the time, the papers only printed the first two courtesy sentences. The splendid Russian poster art has wilted and decayed as rapidly as the art of caricature. The Russian film industry now provides us with " The Whole World Laughs " or with Fascist strong-man idolizations of Peter the Great. Eisenstein, Mandelstamm, Pasternak, Tretiakov and Meyerhold have taught us to what extent creative genius is hampered whenever it runs counter to Stalin's predilections.

Thc old liberal watchword " enrichissez vous " has become the socialist watchword of the Soviet Union, and at the same time the whole chaos of private initiative has re-entered into its national economy.

It is clear that there is no room for Stakhanovism in a truly scientific scheme of planned production. In a properly planned working concern, one worker cannot arbitrarily increase the speed of the running belt without putting out of gear the work of the other sections. Similarly, a factory cannot double its production without endangering the raw material supply of other concerns and the equilibrium of the market. In the long run, therefore, the Stakhanov system must result in fresh chaos ; the planned economy must explode from inside. Undoubtedly the rise in the standard of living of the bureaucracy and of the working class aristocracy has been miraculous during the last four years, but it is also a fact that, even after the critical year 1932, the standard of living of the unskilled masses continues to be lower than that of the unemployed in Poland.

In large modern steamers we sailed from Sochi to Sevastopol and from Sevastopol to Odessa. In the first-class saloon there was dancing till late into the night, but on deck it was impossible to move without stumbling upon human beings who day and night were sitting and lying about occupying literally every inch of the space. They were dressed in rags and for the whole duration of the voyage, which lasted from two to three days, they had nothing to eat but brown bread and some unripe plums. When asked why they were on the move, they invariably replied that famine reigned in their village during the Winter, and that they were forced to try and earn something along the coast during the Summer. While it is correct that prices have dropped considerably in the open market, it must be pointed out that, whereas wages for the lowest groups have remained the same, these open market prices amount to about double the old prices in the closed shops. It is easy to brag about the rise in wages in Soviet Union, but it should be added that the devaluation of the rouble was officially recognized when it was brought down from 1.50 florin to 30 cents. Apart from a few exceptional prices and charges—books, newspapers and railway tickets occur to one's mind—the actual purchasing power of the rouble is nearer five than ten Dutch cents, and even so tram fares in Moscow have doubled, while at the same time a zone tariff has been introduced. A ticket in the famous underground costs one rouble. How often can the fare be paid by a worker earning 100 roubles a month?

Indirect wages, as they are called, have also become more and more limited in scope. Since 1935, even medicaments have again to be paid for in the Soviet chemists' shops. It is now the exception to have access to urban parks without payment and, whereas formerly one could bathe in the Moscow river free of charge, one now has to pay 65 copeks for the obligatory swimming establishment and the hiring of bathing drawers. Theatrical performances have also ceased to be free. Such examples could be multiplied indefinitely.

It has been suggested that present conditions in the Soviet Union viewed in themselves are no more fraught with peril than those obtaining during the New Economic Policy period in the days of Lenin. This is correct, and it is equally true that the cultural life of the Soviet Union is still permeated through and through with a genuine socialist spirit. The results of the revolution cannot be undone in a few years. There is still so much that is worth while seeing in the Soviet Union that whoever visits the country for the first time—and is therefore not in a position to draw comparisons with an earlier period—returns full of enthusiasm. But whereas the N.E.P. period was considered at the time as a necessary though retrograde step, the present reaction is represented to us as the only real socialist ideal, which can be criticized only at one's peril. The power of the State is directed not against the N.E.P. traders, but against the dissolved union of combatants in the civil war, against the union of old Bolsheviks, against the youth leaders of Leningrad, against revolutionary writers, such as Tarassov, Rodianov, Tretiakov, Mandelstamm, against revolutionary theatrical managers such as Eisenstein and Meierhold. It is directed against all the members of the old revolutionary government in Russia and the autonomous states, against the creators of the revolutionary army, and the revolutionary air force, against the ambassadors who were pursuing the Soviet's revolutionary policy abroad. Indeed, in the matter of executions, the Soviet Union has this year overtaken and surpassed all the other States in the world. Even if it were true that all the military chiefs were agents of Japan, all the leaders of large scale industry, saboteurs, and the best publicists, traitors, what is one to think of a régime that has driven to treason all the big figures of the revolution ?

But, it will be asked, does the new Soviet Constitution offer no guarantees ? It is enough to read the paragraph relating to the right of asylum and then to confront it with the expulsion of hundreds of German and Austrian refugees in the course of this year, and with the arrest of a number of the best comrades (Ottwald, Günther, Zensl, Mühsam) to make one realize how much the true state of affairs diverges from these paper guarantees. This constitution, which is being cried up as the most democratic in the world, cannot bear comparison with the Dutch constitution, in the matter of democratic guarantees. It is only necessary to consider the position with regard to Parliamentary immunity, the right to control finance, Parliamentary rights of initiative and inquiry, the relationship between the two chambers, and the number of times Parliament meets. One need only compare the guaranteed freedom of the press with the actual state of affairs in which even in the artistic sphere no individual tendencies or opinions are allowed. Indeed, if one looks into the new electoral system, where only one candidate is allowed for each electoral list, not much difference will be found between this system and the electoral system of Mussolini's Parliament or of Hitler's Reichstag. A comparison of the new Soviet constitution—assuming that it is to be taken seriously at all—with the old cannot fail to show that it constitutes a tremendous step backwards, and the complete abandonment of Lenin's system of Soviets. Marxism considers the peasants, who are landowners as well as land-labourers, as a hybrid class in which reactionary and revolutionary tendencies are equally divided. In the event of an alliance between peasants and town labourers it demands, therefore, that the proletariat should be predominant. But now the Soviet agricultural system has been modified to this extent : the peasant, apart from being a " collective " peasant, has become once more a peasant on his own, with his own private land and cattle (means of production in private possession !), and an increasingly greater portion of his working hours is withdrawn from the community and devoted to his own small business. Should the agricultural population increase, this development can only lead either to the splitting up of the communal lands among the ever more numerous members, or to the rise of an agricultural proletariat. The new constitution, however, proclaims equality between the town labourers and the peasants at the very moment when this development is taking place !

This reversal is of such far-reaching importance that it would have led to fierce discussion in any other country. A discussion of sorts did take place in the Soviet press ; it even lasted for months. I followed it from day to day and while I noted all the Byzantine flatteries addressed to Stalin, I failed to discover so much as two lines of fundamental principles or, among the thousands of suggestions made, one that was of importance to socialist theory.

Whereas Socialism is the road to human freedom in the sense that it encourages personal responsibility and individual judgment, Fascism is the road taken by all who evade this responsibility and their own judgment. The desire for a leader is the desire of God's children for a protecting, all-wise father, the infantile desire to be a child once more and to be allowed to feel again a father's chastising love. While in 1932 thousands of athletes in the Red Square formed with their bodies the letters

K. I., and, in 1934, the letters U. S. S. R., in 1936 their bodies shaped the word STALIN.

" We thank you, Stalin, for having given us back the joy of living ! " To the socialist idea, to their own strength, they are no longer beholden. The airman who flies across the Pole to America attributes his safe arrival to the fact that he had Stalin constantly in mind, after the fashion of a good Catholic who thinks of the Virgin Mary. It can only be assumed that the other airman who crashed in his Polar expedition was a Trotskyist who was thinking of the devil incarnate, instead of having his mind upon his elevator. All this is pure Fascist ideology and it is not surprising that in every field the same seeds are now bearing forth the same fruits. The Russian trials are a copy of the German events of June 30th, just as Hitler copied the Tuchachevsky episode in getting rid of his own generals.

The view may be taken that the Russians must find salvation in their own way and that the Russian question has precious little to do with a book on Spain. It should not be forgotten, however, that Russia is dominant in the Third International, and that Russian influence is decisive for the policy of the national parties. The history of the last decade has been a long concatenation of errors, changes of course, and defeats. All this was done without the concurrence of the members of the Parties, who were excluded from all influence in matters of policy and who had to rely upon their party paper to find out which of the leaders had been superannuated, and to what extent they had to pursue a line one day which was the opposite of what had to be affirmed the day before. The betrayal complex has been rampant ; party life has been transformed into a Jesuit's court, in which everybody spies upon everybody else, betraying and worming out secrets which perhaps will one day be included in the dossier of one's comrade of yesterday. From excess of idealism the hundred per cent party comrade is prepared in twenty-four hours to disown and betray his best friend. One of the principal activities of the secret Russian G.P.U. in Spain was to imprison, torture, and often kill volunteers of the opposition parties, with the intention of ferreting out what their relations were with the so-called Trotskyists abroad who could then be handed to the Gestapo.

The policy pursued by the Third International, and not only in Spain, is to a great extent Russian State policy. It may therefore serve a useful purpose to analyse this Russian foreign policy.

The policy of the Third International can be defended up to a point by maintaining that for years it was exclusively bent upon the maintenance of the Soviet Union ; to ensure the peaceful completion of the first five-year plan, even the somewhat equivocal German revolution had to be sacrificed. This policy explains the re-arming of the German Reichswehr, the negotiations with its general staff and the extremely friendly relations with Fascist Italy and with an equally Fascist Turkey. There are, however, two conceivable ways of defending the Soviet Union. The first consists in leaning upon the foreign proletariat which, in the event of an attack upon Russia, would launch a civil war against its own ruling class. The other possibility is that of an alliance with capitalist governments. Naturally, in this case, every revolutionary movement among Russia's imperialist allies would have to be excluded. Since the catastrophe in China, where the revolutionary movement of the masses was first sacrificed to the Bourgeois Kuomintang, and betrayed later by Chiang-Kai-Shek, the Soviet Union has exclusively pursued the latter path, which culminated in its entry in the League of Nations. After having maintained their heroic struggle for ten years without the help of Russia, the Chinese Soviets have now sacrificed the results already obtained upon orders from Moscow and have placed their army at the disposal of Chiang-Kai-Shek, who in 1927, in Shanghai alone, was responsible for the death of 11,000 of their comrades. The Chinese people to-day are not fighting for their own social liberation ; they are defending against Japan the interests of the most rapacious imperialism on earth, that of Anglo-Saxon capitalists.

It is not by any means certain that Chiang-Kai-Shek will not commit an act of betrayal a second time, or that the Chinese Bourgeoisie will not make its peace with Japan, in which case the teeming millions of China will become free to fight a war against the Soviet Union. In Spain, it seemed for a time as if Russia would pursue another and better policy, and, so long as I trusted to appearances, I was not only silent myself but also endeavoured to restrain my friend André Gide. Whether Russia's help in Spain has been adequate or whether it has been fatal will be revealed by history rather than by what I have written. One thing, however, is clear : the Communist party in Spain has made every effort to hamper a revolutionary development. Similarly, in every other country, it shows a preference for linking up with the Bourgeois reaction, while it subordinates to fleeting party interest all considerations of comradeship, good faith, honesty, and humanity.

I consider the Church the most dangerous instrument of reaction upon earth. In my view the escape to God is the same escape from oneself which carries us into the arms of the "leader." But I am also aware of having more in common with an honest young Catholic or with an open-minded Protestant than with a Communist who without qualms of conscience and without further thought destroys his comrade of yesterday. The decline of the Communist movement has taught me the absolute necessity of keeping alive a certain number of moral principles.

I do not believe in a personal God, but I believe it is necessary to revere godliness upon earth, as it reveals itself in beauty, justice, freedom, truth, and love. These conceptions are indeed eternal, and Marxism does no more than explain and interpret their various transient shapes and permutations. All we shall gain by forming a hypocritical and opportunist alliance with clericalism is that we shall alienate the genuine, revolutionary youth of believers for whom clericalism is the worst enemy of all.

He who controls the youth of a country controls its future. In Germany, the triumph of Fascism was due to the hold it had obtained over youth. In Spain, on the other hand, it was the youth of the nation that stood in the vanguard of the struggle against Fascism. In Holland, again, the Communist party has dissolved its youth movement, and is now endeavouring by means of dough-nut binges and displays to capture the young in an association catering for their amusement and reaction. The Social Democrats and other sections are meeting with similar difficulties. There must be a reason for this desertion of youth.

Marxism is an excellent working hypothesis for economic research : indeed its economic premises are confirmed more clearly every day. But it is also something more : it points to practical ways and means for achieving the material foundations of a Communist society. On the other hand, it falls short in the psychological field and is handicapped by the scientific limitations of the time in which it arose.

Nobody has ever become a socialist on purely rational grounds. Nobody has sacrificed his life for purely rational considerations. The roots of socialism spring from humanitarianism and lay in the human heart for many centuries before Marx appeared.

Historical materialism is working for the future mastery of the spirit by means of those material resources which until now have restricted and dominated this spirit. If in the process it postulates the importance of the forces of production, it is because these forces are necessary to satisfy one of the basic human needs : hunger. As a consequence, two other equally fundamental human instincts were thrust by Marxism into the background : Freud speaks of an urge towards death marching side by side with the urge towards life. This urge is explained by Reich as a desire to flow back into the universe, a parallel to the sexual act. It seems to me that this urge towards death is partly responsible for one of the most characteristic traits of youth, its desire for self-sacrifice. I have already pointed to the error committed by the Socialist movement in endeavouring to attract young people primarily by appealing to their interests. Youth is irrational and has to prove its worth to itself and to others by courage and nobility. Certainly, it will not be gainsaid that socialism has at all times exacted the heaviest sacrifices from its adherents. But, whereas the Socialist movement assumed this factor to be too self-evident to be stressed, the Fascists by their monster propaganda have made it appear as if they alone held in fee this capacity for self-sacrifice.

People talk of crisis and revolution ; the real crisis, however, was present long before the economic crisis, and the real revolution began long before the Russian Revolution. The Jewish persecutions of the present day and the outcry against a Judaic Christianity are not a pure manœuvre ; they constitute the foolish and intuitive manifestation of a hatred which is directed against individuals, although aimed in effect at a particular conception of life. The Jewish faith was the first religion to declare that God was spirit ; if the Jewish people have a national mission in the history of the world, this mission must be the spreading of internationalism. The Jews were the first world citizens and were in the position to be so because their God was no national god, but the spirit itself, which in truth is international. Christianity took over this majestic conception. Catholicism knows no peoples and no races ; Christ gave his blood to show that blood is not the highest good, and that all men are brothers in the spirit.

This victory over the national gods was a tremendous step forward. Nevertheless, the fact that the new God, who was spirit only, was bereft of body was a retrograde step. Body and spirit were no longer equally godly as in the days of Hellas. On the contrary, the new god was a jealous god, who demanded that all the lusts of the flesh should be sublimated in the spirit. The whole course of Christian civilization has been a perpetual struggle against the flesh and the sexual instincts ; a war against the forces of nature has lasted for centuries and could only be won by magnifying man's sense of sin into a neurosis. While it would be foolish to deny to what cultural and spiritual heights this sublimation has occasionally led, it is painfully clear that this condemnation of the sexual instinct—

which incidentally was a necessary consequence of the rights of property and the institution of the family—has poisoned the very root from which we draw our lives.

The crisis set in with the Rationalists and the French Revolution, as soon as the belief of the masses in hell and purgatory had begun to wane. Rousseau, the *poètes damnés*, sport, the night life of big cities, realism, the rise of sexual literature, camping, the Nudist movement, the Boy Scout movement, the new Paganism (which was prevalent long before the Nazis resuscitated Wotan) have been only so many symptoms of the confused and still largely unconscious revolt of the masses.

The pastor of Urk, who considers football immoral because of the players' bare knees, is fundamentally as much in the right as Franco's priests who are again forbidding children to paddle on the Basque coast. The flesh itself is deemed to be sinful. At the same time owing to economic circumstance the youth of the present day have fewer and fewer opportunities for leading a normal sexual life, and in this respect are anything but saintly. Their sexual need is great as can be seen by opening almost any of the recent war books, where under a thin veneer of pacifism the author's yearning for the miserable erotic surrogates provided by comradeship in the trenches is clearly revealed.

German National Socialism has grown great by exploiting in a psychologically masterly fashion these confused sexual needs which are still steeped in a sense of sin. Here too, however, as in every other field, it has only surrogates to offer in the form of masculine associations, hysterical gatherings, and the exploitation of masochist and sadist instincts.

Communism, on the other hand, has nothing at all to offer. Without further inquiry it rejects equally the present-day epicurean doctrines of André Gide and the scientific results of Reich's investigations. In the moral sphere it has fallen back upon the puritanism of the bleakest of Protestant sects. And, meanwhile, the youth of the world, bereft of all leadership, is endeavouring to anæsthetize itself with sport, the craze for motoring, dancing, and wireless, in so far as it has not already succumbed to Fascist watchwords, which can only give meaning to a meaningless existence by offering death for the fatherland.

One becomes infatuated with abstractions when one is afraid or unable to care for human beings. These abstractions are called parties or ideals, and in their name life becomes dehumanized. Never has life meant so little as in these times of vociferous ideals, and yet it is only necessary to keep one's ear to the ground to become aware that everywhere and in all circles the same current of opinion is beginning to gather strength, and that already a new front is about to be constituted which will cut across all parties.

It has long been customary to look upon Hitler and Mussolini as paranoiacs—in which case we have deserved the contumely which attaches to being defeated by paranoiacs. In actual fact, Hitler and Mussolini have sensed more clearly than many of our leaders what has been brewing among the masses. We have considered all Hitler's adherents as self-seeking scamps, and in so doing have affronted the working-class from whose ranks have sprung many of Hitler's most earnest and idealistic adherents. We have rejected Fascism lock, stock, and barrel, and in so doing have denied ourselves an insight into the very real qualities of Fascism, which appealed and still appeal to the masses.

There is no more unity in Fascism than in the Russian Revolution. It is a synthesis of action and reaction, of truths and falsehoods, in which the falsehoods predominate. Fascism is on the one hand a truly revolutionary, though blind, protest of the masses, and, on the other hand, an imposture of the leaders, who are endeavouring to capture this protest and to make it subserve the interests of the *status quo*, the interests of the lower middle class, and those of large-scale capitalists. The official Fascist press is unequalled in the world for its barbarity and fraudulent mendacity, but in such books as *The Third Reich*, in the organs of the "Black Front" and even here and there in the press of the present-day German Youth Movement, one hits upon many expressions and thoughts that might have been set down in the trenches outside Madrid. Unfortunately, owing to our refusal to study Fascism with scientific objectivity, we debar ourselves from gaining access to a Fascist youth which, once won over, would rise up on our side against its leaders.

What I have written will no doubt be considered as a broadside against official Communists. Such, however, was never my intention. On the contrary I have everywhere attempted to the best of my ability to stress the positive services which the Communists have rendered and the motives by which they have been actuated.

To the Communist youth belongs the imperishable honour of having taken the initiative in organizing the International Brigades at the front of Madrid. In the International Brigades its best members have fought. The word, international, was turned into a thing of flesh and blood, and the international working class youth were given a deathless example of heroism.

This book is a book about Spain. It claims to be the book of a combatant who even now refuses to lay down his arms. Meanwhile, the Spanish youth battling on the front of humanity are still struggling for freedom, and the issue will decide the fate of Europe.

I am confident that they will be triumphant. But even if they should temporarily go under, owing to an even greater betrayal of the democratic countries, the struggle will not have been in vain. For centuries, it will serve as a beacon and an encouragement to the working-classes; for the proletariat, only those defeats are disastrous which have been endured without a struggle.

Aware of the profound enthusiasm and the incredible powers of resistance of our Spanish comrades, I do not believe that it will come to that. Nevertheless, no sacrifice can be too heavy and no action superfluous in order to support our comrades at the front. It is necessary for the entire youth of the world to unite in the struggle for the future. The solution lies not in a united front based upon opportunism, nor in a Fourth International in which the old dogmas will be interpreted in some new fashion. Our united front must embrace all who feel the spirit of comradeship, whatsoever the party to which they may belong; it must include all who are prepared to carry on the struggle without any thought of private gain and without any reservation. It must be the united front of all who realize that we possess no stronger weapon than the truth. Only by such a united front can Fascism be broken. It must be broken, not only in its material strength, but also in its all-pervading spirit of corruption, by which races and peoples are separated instead of being drawn together in a common love for humanity.

Let us recover our right to love, our right to our own opinion, our right to respect. Let us even respect the enemy when his integrity is not in doubt.

9780415853064